RICHARD GATLIN AND THE CONFEDERATE DEFENSE OF EASTERN NORTH CAROLINA

JAMES L. GADDIS JR.

THE History PRESS

Published by The History Press
Charleston, SC 29403
www.historypress.net

Front cover, top: Richard C. Gatlin as North Carolina adjutant general. *North Carolina Museum of History*.
Front cover, bottom: General view of Forts Hatteras and Clark, from *Frank Leslie's Illustrated Newspaper*, September 14, 1861. *North Carolina County Photographic Collection #P0001, Wilson Library, University of North Carolina–Chapel Hill.*
Back cover, top: Federal troops occupying captured Confederate fortifications near New Bern in March 1862. *North Carolina Archives*.
Back cover, bottom: Oil portrait of Richard C. Gatlin at about age eighty. *North Carolina Museum of History*.

First published 2015

Manufactured in the United States

ISBN 978.1.62619.842.5

Library of Congress Control Number: 2014956643

Richard C. Gatlin as adjutant general of North Carolina. *North Carolina Museum of History*.

Contents

Preface

For most of the critical first year of the American Civil War, Richard Caswell Gatlin (1809–1896) was the highest-ranking Confederate officer in the state of North Carolina. Even so, historians have mentioned him only casually, if at all, in most North Carolina Civil War literature. I discovered Gatlin while thumbing through the *Historical Times Illustrated Encyclopedia of the Civil War*, in which I spotted a short biography that began, "Richard Caswell Gatlin, CSA, b. Lenoir Cty., N.C." Although Gatlin's name was new to me, his birthplace, Lenoir County, North Carolina, has been home to at least one line of my family since colonial days, so I eagerly read on. I found that Gatlin grew up in Kinston, Lenoir County's largest town and the scene of two Civil War battles, and that, as a brigadier general in the Provisional Army of the Confederate States, he commanded the defending Confederate forces when most of eastern North Carolina succumbed to a Federal invasion in 1862. Although relatively well versed in Lenoir County history, especially its Civil War history, I was unaware that Lenoir County was the birthplace of a Confederate general. In fact, in his epic work *Bethel to Sharpsburg*, D.H. Hill mistakenly notes that Gatlin was a native of Perquimans County, North Carolina.

Now intensely curious about Gatlin, I asked local historians about him, but to my surprise, few were familiar with him. Some thought I meant Richard J. Gatling, the North Carolinian who invented the Gatling gun. Perplexed that a Confederate general remained unheralded in a hometown and county that abound with pride in their Civil War history, and that once were the front line of the Confederacy, I dug deeper.

Gatlin's grandfather, as I soon learned, was Richard Caswell—Kinston's founder and favorite son, a Revolutionary War general and North Carolina's first constitutional governor. Gatlin's parents were early residents of Kinston, but Gatlin's father died in 1836 and his mother in 1843. Two of Gatlin's four sisters died before 1840; the other two sisters married and moved away in 1837. Gatlin's only brother, an army surgeon, perished in the Dade Massacre in Florida in 1835. Uncles, aunts, nieces and nephews had followed the cotton trail to Georgia, Alabama, Tennessee and Arkansas. Gatlin left Kinston at age nineteen to attend the United States Military Academy at West Point. He never lived in Kinston again, although he returned many times on business and pleasure and always considered himself a Kinstonian. No Gatlin family descendants remained in the Kinston area in the generations after 1840 to remind Kinstonians that Richard Caswell Gatlin was one of their own. These details, and the fact that historians have almost universally relegated Gatlin's Civil War activities to footnote status, might help explain why he achieved only scant recognition in eastern North Carolina and elsewhere.

Sadly, time and circumstance have obscured much of Kinston and Lenoir County's nineteenth-century history. Because fires in 1878, 1880 and 1895 destroyed virtually all the county's early deeds and historical records,[1] leaving little primary data at hand, historians suffer a dearth of information about local personalities of the eighteenth and nineteenth centuries. Published studies of Kinston's past have generally focused on the fabled Richard Caswell, the town's two Civil War battles and the Confederate ironclad gunboat CSS *Neuse*. Gatlin was, however, the proverbial hometown boy made good. He traveled extensively across the rugged American frontier. He pioneered, soldiered and saw things that few people of his time could have imagined. Much of Gatlin's intrigue stems from his association with other nineteenth-century American personalities, military leaders, explorers, artists, writers, governors, presidents and the like. He lived among many whose names and lives are still familiar to some of us, names like Edgar Allan Poe, Winfield Scott, Nathan Boone, Washington Irving, George Catlin, B.L.E. Bonneville, Zachary Taylor, Jim Bridger, Jefferson Davis, Robert E. Lee, Braxton Bragg, Governor Zebulon Vance, "Hanging" Judge Isaac Parker and hosts of others. Gatlin lived for eighty-seven years, nearly the entirety of the nineteenth century. During the twenty-nine years he served as an officer in the U.S. Seventh Infantry, he and his fellow soldiers endured Florida's steamy hammocks, Mexico's exotic valleys, Wyoming's frozen peaks and an astounding array of stagecoach, horseback, steamboat and railroad treks across a United States that reached for and achieved its

Manifest Destiny. In his lifetime, Gatlin saw the young United States grow from seventeen eastern seaboard states to forty-six states stretching from the Atlantic to the Pacific. He experienced the country's emergence from a small nation of independent farmers to an industrialized giant. Thomas Jefferson was president when Gatlin was born. William McKinley was nearing election when Gatlin died.

Gatlin was a terse communicator and not a prolific writer. He left no diary or journal, but he did leave a smattering of personal letters and a brief memoir written in September 1861. The Southern Collection at the Wilson Library at UNC–Chapel Hill houses his small collection of papers. I was fortunate to find a few facts about him from U.S. Army regimental and post returns, from the U.S. Adjutant General Letters found at Fold3 and from the North Carolina Adjutant General Letter Book at the State Archives in Raleigh. I learned much about his role in the Civil War from the *Official Records of the War of Rebellion*.

This work, in part, explores Gatlin's activities from North Carolina's secession in May 1861 through the fall of New Bern in March 1862. Gatlin and his fellow defenders devoted that period to developing eastern North Carolina's defensive works along its three-hundred-mile coastline, at first to repulse a Union invasion and later to keep the Union in check on the Outer Banks. However, a severe shortage of men and arms, a woefully inadequate navy, significant Union sentiment among the coastal residents, a Federal army and navy poised to attack at virtually any point it chose and the failure of the Confederate government to support its North Carolina generals undermined those efforts. Narratives of this period usually feature the names of Governor John Ellis, Governor Henry Toole Clark and Brigadier Generals D.H. Hill and Lawrence O'Bryan Branch, but Hill and Branch were under Gatlin's command and acted at Gatlin's direction.

The remainder of this work encapsulates Gatlin's experiences leading to and following his brief Confederate service. I hope readers of history, Civil War historians and the people of eastern North Carolina in particular will come to know Gatlin through these pages. So many of Gatlin's important nineteenth-century American military exploits could be more fully explored than I have done in this biography, but because the ten-month period he devoted to defending eastern North Carolina cemented a special place for him in North Carolina history, much of this work is devoted to that period.

Gatlin achieved much during his lifetime, rose to nearly the top of his military profession and watched his world crumble in a few short months. He experienced a fair share of tragedy in his personal life, but he persevered

Brigadier General Richard C. Gatlin's Confederate frock coat and U.S. Army officer's sword. *North Carolina Museum of History.*

under conditions that today might seem intolerable. He was an exemplar of southern pride and honor. Significantly for Kinston and for Lenoir County, and for all of eastern North Carolina, one of the most notable soldiers of the Civil War and before was one of its own sons: Richard Caswell Gatlin.

Acknowledgements

The most valuable contributor to this work has been my very patient and helpful wife, Suzanne Rose Gaddis. She trekked with me to myriad libraries, bookstores and historic sites. She waded through books, archives, websites, letters and journals. Most importantly, she had a sense for determining what was meaningful and significant in Gatlin's life. To her, I give my greatest thanks.

Early in the project, the late Dr. Keats Sparrow, then dean of the Thomas Harriot School of Arts and Sciences at East Carolina University, took an interest in this work and offered support and encouragement.

Mrs. Nancy Cobb Lilly of Raleigh grew up under the loving eye of her step-grandmother, Mary Knox Gatlin Cobb, Richard C. Gatlin's youngest daughter. As the closest living link to Gatlin, Mrs. Lilly has been insightful and inspirational.

I am grateful to three excellent historians and authors: Michael C. Hardy, Walter C. Hilderman III and Matthew Poteat, each of whom carefully read and critiqued my manuscript, much to my delight and to the story's betterment.

To all these folks and dozens of others who patiently listened to my tales of Gatlin, I offer my sincere and heartfelt thanks.

Prologue

"Specter of Yankees": Disaster at New Bern

As cannon fire burst closer, hundreds of New Bern's terror-stricken people clutched their belongings, clambered onto trains, scurried into wagons and coaches, leapt onto horses and escaped westward to safety. They fled the oncoming Burnside Expedition, the despised blue-coated Union army that, five weeks earlier, had overwhelmed Roanoke Island and that now, after thundering into the town of New Bern, ruled most of the North Carolina coast.

On March 14, 1862, the specter of Yankees occupying New Bern washed across eastern North Carolina like a September hurricane. One day earlier, General Ambrose P. Burnside's twelve-thousand-man Federal armada had steamed through North Carolina's Pamlico Sound and landed on the mainland below the Confederate defenses at New Bern. The invaders then drove out the determined but meager Confederate resistance before them. In a grinding, four-hour battle, the Yankees captured New Bern, the state's second-largest port city.[2]

Stunned and staggering, remnants of a four-thousand-man Confederate army fled westward, too. They halted at the railroad town of Kinston, the nearest point of refuge, thirty-five miles west of New Bern and thirty miles east of Goldsboro, where commanding Brigadier General Richard C. Gatlin maintained the headquarters of the Confederate Department of North Carolina. In Kinston, Gatlin's subordinate, Brigadier General Lawrence O'Bryan Branch, who had been the commanding general at New Bern, and Brigadier General Samuel G. French, newly arrived from Virginia, prepared

Battle of New Bern, March 14, 1862, as illustrated in *Harper's Weekly*, April 5, 1862.

to beat back a massive Yankee push that appeared imminent. Burnside's late-winter amphibious campaign had given the Union a significant victory over the Confederacy and control over North Carolina's coastal sounds and rivers. Now at the back door to the South's shipbuilding and munitions center at Norfolk, the Union army appeared primed to both invade southern Virginia and to penetrate North Carolina to capture the vital Wilmington & Weldon Railroad, which supplied the Confederate capital at Richmond.[3]

Chapter 1

"Cope of Heaven": Caswells, Gatlins and Kinston

In 1585, English explorer and colonist Ralph Lane described the coastal plain of present-day North Carolina as "the goodliest soile under the cope of Heaven."[4] Despite Lane's glowing endorsement, the English were slow to work their way into eastern North Carolina. The treacherous Graveyard of the Atlantic, the Outer Banks, guarded most of the North Carolina mainland, while the Chesapeake Bay and Charleston Harbor made putting in at Virginia and South Carolina more inviting and judicious for seagoing merchant ships and immigrants.

Still, spillover from Virginia was inevitable. By 1696, that part of North Carolina south of the Albemarle Sound and north of Cape Fear was populous enough to warrant its designation as Bath County. On the Pamlico River in 1706, Bath Town became the first town in present-day North Carolina. In 1710, Baron Christoff Von Graffenreid brought a colony of Swiss Palatines into North Carolina to establish the town of New Bern where the Neuse River begins to widen into the Pamlico Sound. In that first decade of the eighteenth century, a migratory wave swelled southward to the Pamlico and Neuse River Valleys in such numbers that Bath County reorganized in 1712 into Craven, Beaufort and Hyde Counties.[5]

Adventurers and settlers from coastal North Carolina pushed westward up the Neuse River Valley. They and others from the northern North Carolina counties began arriving upriver from New Bern as early as 1729. The Neuse River was navigable up to and well beyond a small feeder stream known as Atkins Branch, some thirty-five miles west of New Bern. Because of its ready access to the river trade, settlers remained in the Atkins Branch area after the 1740s. In 1756, Royal Governor Arthur Dobbs purchased a tract of land near Atkins Branch and named it Tower Hill. Some inspired pioneers planned the town of George City at Tower Hill in 1758, but a more desirable location a little farther upstream at a bend on the Neuse River became the town of Kingston in 1762. In 1783, in a symbolic act of defiance to the Crown after the colonies had won their independence from Great Britain, the people of Kingston dropped the letter "g" and adopted the unusual town name of Kinston.[6]

From 1747 to 1789, the Kinston area was home to Richard Caswell, North Carolina's first constitutional governor. Born in 1729 in Joppa, Maryland, young Richard Caswell had journeyed with his family to New Bern in the 1740s and sought a royal position. In 1747, Caswell began an apprenticeship with North Carolina surveyor-general and assemblyman James Mackilwain and took up residence at Mackilwain's plantation near present-day Kinston. In 1752, he married Mackilwain's daughter, Mary, and began acquiring a substantial quantity of land. After Mary died in childbirth in 1757, Caswell married Sarah Herritage, daughter of William Herritage, a lawyer, clerk of the general assembly and owner of a large plantation named Harrow in the Woodington section of today's Lenoir County. The people of North Carolina elected Caswell to the colony's general assembly in 1754. He served in that post for the next twenty-two years while gradually adding to his holdings in and around Kinston. By 1775, Caswell was one of the largest landowners in the area.

In 1771, Caswell commanded one of Royal Governor Tryon's militia units in suppressing the "Regulator Movement" in Piedmont North Carolina. By the outbreak of the American Revolution in 1775, however, Caswell openly favored independence from Great Britain and formed a local militia unit known as the "Minute Men of Dobbs." On February 27, 1776, Caswell and his minutemen marched seventy miles from New Bern to a small clearing along Moore's Creek near Wilmington, where they and other militia units from eastern North Carolina intercepted and destroyed a column of Loyalist Highland Scots at a place called Moore's Creek Bridge. The American victory at Moore's Creek Bridge effectively put an end to organized Loyalist resistance in North Carolina and secured the colony for the Patriots' cause.

In 1776, following the signing of the Declaration of Independence, Caswell became North Carolina's first post-colonial governor, and his residence at Kinston became the de facto state capitol. Caswell served four consecutive one-year terms as governor, from 1776 to 1780, and three more terms from

1784 through 1787. While serving as a state legislator from Dobbs County in the new state capital of Fayetteville, he suddenly collapsed and died in 1789. Following a funeral in Fayetteville, according to legend, a formal procession escorted his body to Kinston, where the family interred him in the graveyard on his Red House Plantation. As distinguished as Richard Caswell's public life was, tragedy pierced his personal life. He had nine children from two marriages, but two of his children died in infancy, and only three lived to old age.

Caswell's daughter, Susannah Caswell, was born on February 17, 1775, one year before her famous father led the "Minute Men of Dobbs" in the stunning victory over the Tories at the Battle of Moore's Creek Bridge. In 1794, nineteen-year-old Susannah married her first cousin John Lovick, moved into a house on the corner of Herritage and Shine Streets in Kinston and resided there for the next six years.[7]

Edward Gatlin was born at Isle of Wight, Virginia, about 1680, son of William Gatlin, a native-born Englishman who had migrated to America. Around the year 1700, Edward went into coastal North Carolina and somehow survived the Tuscarora Indian uprising that nearly destroyed New Bern and the surrounding settlements in 1711. By the late 1730s, Edward's son John Gatlin had married and had four sons, one of whom was Thomas Gatlin, born in 1740. Thomas Gatlin's son, another John Gatlin, was born on January 10, 1769. Around 1795, this young John Gatlin, in his mid-twenties, moved upriver to Kinston.

By 1800, Kinston had become the county seat of Lenoir County. The town amounted to just a few muddy, rutted streets dotted with about a dozen frame houses and ten families. The promising village that, sixteen years earlier, had dropped the "g" from its name in defiance to the king of England and that, a quarter of a century before, had been the capital of North Carolina had progressed little since its founding. Even so, Kinston was a quaint, pleasant little town. Nestled on a steep bank of the Neuse River, it drifted along slowly with the river and the times.

The ambitious and enterprising John Gatlin had come to Kinston from Craven County in the mid-1790s and had successfully established himself as a man of great promise. Gatlin succeeded John Lovick as Kinston's postmaster in 1797, and Gatlin's brother, Slade Gatlin, assumed that same post in 1800. As neighbors in the tiny village of Kinston, John Lovick and John Gatlin were friends and fellow members of the Saint John's Masonic Lodge. In 1801, John Lovick died unexpectedly. John Gatlin married the young widow Susannah Caswell Lovick the following year and, in 1803, moved with his new bride and two stepchildren to the Red House Plantation, the late Governor Caswell's one-time home about two miles up the Neuse River west of Kinston.

As a farmer, merchant and owner of eighteen slaves in 1810, John Gatlin was quite well off. He and Susannah became parents of five children. In the dead of winter, on January 18, 1809, their third child, Richard Caswell Gatlin, was born at the Red House Plantation.[8] Young Richard spent his first six years at the Red House Plantation listening to tales of his storied grandfather's Revolutionary War adventures. He and his elder brother, John Slade Gatlin, undoubtedly spent many a day down along the Neuse River, which ran beside the Red House Plantation. The river was an exciting place for the two young boys to grow up. It flowed past the Red House on an almost northerly course and then bent to the southeast before snaking its way to the town of Kinston. It is not difficult to envision Richard Gatlin scrambling down its banks to swim and fish and to watch canoes and rafts glide past. Flatboats and barges had once been a common sight on the Neuse, plying their way upriver nearly to what is today Smithfield and then

The Capps house in Kinston near the Red House Plantation, possible birthplace of R.C. Gatlin. *Author's collection.*

back down to New Bern, hauling grain, livestock, lumber, imports and other goods. But the boats were not as numerous in the 1810s as they had been a few years earlier.

The Gatlin family maintained the Red House Plantation and increased their slaveholdings to twenty-five by 1820,[9] but in 1815, they moved to a cottage in Kinston on the northeast corner of East Bright and Mackilwain (now McLewean) Streets. John Gatlin became increasingly successful in his trade ventures, one of which was the retailing of "spiriteous liquor."[10] The eldest child, eleven-year-old Susan Jefferson Gatlin, died in 1814, but the four remaining Gatlin children grew up well educated by standards of the time and place. John and Richard attended the New Bern Academy for at least part of their formal schooling.

Chapter 2

"God-Forsaken Place": West Point

In 1824, at age fifteen, Richard Gatlin and his elder brother, John, enrolled at the University of North Carolina in Chapel Hill. A year later, both boys were back home with little chance of completing their college-level schooling. John Gatlin evidently could no longer afford to send his sons to college, perhaps due to lingering effects from the economic downturn of 1819.

Richard turned eighteen in 1827 and began to consider attending the United States Military Academy at West Point, New York. The academy offered a free college education to candidates who could secure an appointment, pass the stringent entrance requirements and were willing to devote five years to military service upon graduation. West Point appointments were difficult to achieve. United States senators or congressmen nominated candidates to the secretary of war, and then the secretary of war routed his recommendations to the president of the United States for final appointment. Those young men whose families were politically well connected stood a far better chance of receiving nominations than did the average farm boy. Most appointments went to the sons or grandsons of well-placed public officials, former war heroes and current military officers, those known to or influential with the legislators. Fortunately for Richard, the Gatlin family had connections. John Gatlin launched a campaign to have his son appointed. He wrote to his cousin Representative John H. Bryan in Washington, D.C., on December 27, 1827:

> *My son Richard C. Gatlin has a wish to go to the Military School at West Point. He is in his nineteenth year of his age…be so good as to call at the*

War Office and ascertain whether one of his age can be received and if so procure a place for him if there is a vacancy and let me know as soon as convenient. I have nothing new or interesting to communicate only we have lost a great deal of our meat in consequence of the warmth of the season.[11]

Support for Richard's nomination came from the pillars of Lenoir County society. Former U.S. congressman William Blackledge wrote to both of North Carolina's U.S. senators, John Branch and Nathaniel Macon, extolling the virtues of young Richard Caswell Gatlin and urging them to nominate Gatlin as a tribute to Gatlin's grandfather, Richard Caswell.[12] Others who wrote to Senator Branch on Gatlin's behalf were influential men of the community, including Benjamin Coleman, William Croom, Nathan G. Blount and John Cobb.[13] In February 1828, Richard received an acceptance letter from Secretary of War James Barbour. President John Quincy Adams had provisionally appointed Richard to a cadetship at the military academy and directed him to report to West Point between June and August 1828. Richard replied by mail with the understated emotion that would characterize most of his writing, stating that he would indeed report to West Point at the appointed time, "barring any unforeseen circumstances."[14]

Richard Gatlin left Kinston for New York in June 1828. He traveled in the modes of the day—by stagecoach to Norfolk, by sloop up the Chesapeake Bay to Baltimore, by stagecoach to Philadelphia and New York and by steamboat up the Hudson River, a five-hundred-mile journey. On July 1, 1828, he enrolled at West Point, where he soon became acquainted with upperclassmen Robert E. Lee and Joseph E. Johnston, future Confederate generals, and with many other young cadets who, over the following thirty years, would help shape America's military history. An acquaintance from back home, Theophilus Hunter Holmes, was entering his final year at West Point when Richard arrived as a first-year cadet, or plebe. Holmes was from nearby Sampson County, and his father, Gabriel Holmes, had been governor of North Carolina from 1821 to 1824. Holmes and Richard Gatlin would remain close friends in future years, share military assignments and serve together in both the Seventh U.S. Infantry and the Confederate army.

Shortly after arriving at West Point, Gatlin struck up a friendship with another plebe, Daniel Powers Whiting from New York State. The two new cadets would eventually serve together in the Seventh Infantry, marry sisters and command infantry companies in the Mexican War. They remained bosom friends for thirty-two years until forced to choose opposing sides in the Civil War.

A circa 1848 photo of Edgar Allan Poe, Gatlin's fellow West Point cadet in 1831. *Library of Congress.*

Among Gatlin's other classmates during his four years at West Point was an aspiring young writer from Baltimore named Edgar Allan Poe. Poe's unhappy stay at West Point was brief. Writing to a friend, Poe exclaimed that the only "congenial soul" in the "God-forsaken place" was Irishman Benny Havens, the owner of the local tavern frequented often by cadets. Although probably acquainted with Poe, Gatlin was not among the 131 cadets (a majority of the cadet body) who contributed $1.25 each to help Poe finance and publish a book of poems. Immediately following Poe's expulsion from West Point in 1831, he published *Poems by Edgar A. Poe: Second Edition* and dedicated it to the "U.S. Corps of Cadets."[15]

Arriving at West Point in July 1828 were 64 new cadets, including Richard Gatlin. From the previous year's class, 6 others were required to repeat the first year's coursework, resulting in a total of 70 fourth classmen in 1828. Only 45 of them would complete the grueling academic marathon at the academy in four years, and Richard would be one of those (8 others of Richard's original class would graduate after five years). Academically, in his "plebe" (first) year as a cadet, Richard ranked 52nd among the 70 entering cadets. In 1830, his "yearling," or second year, he ranked 45th of 59 cadets. In his junior year, or "cow year," he was 44th of 52 cadets. Although not a particularly gifted student, Cadet Gatlin graduated after four years on July 1, 1832, 35th in his class of 45 graduates. The thirty-seven demerits he had received in his first year placed him 74th of 156 cadets in that category. He racked up sixty-three demerits in 1830, placing him 93rd out of 215 cadets that academic year. He had only thirty-three demerits in 1831, placing him 52nd out of 219 cadets. He earned seventy-six demerits in 1832, ranking him 123rd out of 211 cadets. Gatlin might have accrued demerits for minor infractions, such as "an unkempt room and deficiencies in uniform appearance,"[16] or more serious disciplinary lapses, but he clearly was not negligent in his academy deportment. In all respects, Gatlin appears to have been an average cadet. In his short memoirs, Gatlin's terse description of his West Point experience was: "Entered Military Academy July 1st 1828 and graduated July 1st 1832. Appointed Bt. 2nd Lieut. in the 7th Infantry July 1st 1832."[17]

Upon graduating, cadets typically took a four-month furlough. As events transpired, much of the class of 1832 would not take a furlough but instead go directly from the academy to war.

Chapter 3

"In Consequence of the Cholera": The Black Hawk War

An 1804 treaty had allowed the Indian tribes of the Old Northwest, notably the Sauk and the Fox, to remain on their Illinois lands until the lands were sold or otherwise disposed of by the federal government. By 1831, the state of Illinois had grown so populous that the Sauk, Fox and other Illinois Indians were directed to move westward across the Mississippi River.[18]

Following a year of exile in Iowa, one segment of the Sauk tribe, led by a tribal chieftain named Black Hawk (1767–1838), chose to return to Illinois and resettle its former town. Black Hawk had gained respect among his people while fighting for the British during the War of 1812. In April 1832, Black Hawk's braves, with their wives and families, numbering four hundred in all, planted corn and so resolutely held fast to their land that Illinois governor John Reynolds called on the militia to evict them. Alarmed by the Indian threat, the militiamen organized quickly, including one unit commanded by young lawyer Abraham Lincoln.[19]

However, President Andrew Jackson, an old Indian fighter himself, interceded. He sent General Henry Atkinson and the U.S. Army to northern Illinois hoping to intimidate the Indians into leaving. Overwhelmed and without allies, Black Hawk agreed to return to Iowa. Before the band of Indians could leave, fighting broke out among the Indians and militia, and some whites and Indians were killed. This unfortunate bloodshed ignited the so-called Black Hawk War. Black Hawk's band vengefully attacked and defeated a larger force of Illinois militia and then escaped into hiding in Wisconsin.[20]

Black Hawk and his followers managed to elude and embarrass the army for a month, frustrating President Jackson in an election year, so in late June 1832, Jackson directed General Winfield Scott, at that time headquartered in New York City, to assume command of the Black Hawk War and bring it to a speedy conclusion. Scott quickly assembled about 850 men, drawing troops from New York State, the northern Border States and from among the artillerists at Fortress Monroe in Virginia. Most of Scott's troops, including future Confederate general First Lieutenant Joseph E. Johnston, prepared for their first taste of armed conflict. Scott daringly arranged for four steamships—the *Henry Clay*, the *Sheldon Thompson*, the *William Penn* and the *Superior*—to transport those troops and himself to Fort Dearborn in Chicago by way of Lake Erie, Lake Huron and Lake Michigan. Steamers had never plied the Great Lakes waters for such a distance, but Scott was

An undated photo of Winfield Scott, Gatlin's longtime army commander. *Library of Congress.*

confident that it was the best and quickest way to rush the needed men and supplies to the seat of the Black Hawk War.

Thinking it would be an excellent firsthand learning experience for them, Scott urged members of the West Point class of 1832 to accompany his campaign. Gatlin was among the seventeen graduates who elected to join Scott in New York City. The Scott battalion steamed up the Hudson River to Albany and took flatboats across the Erie Canal to Buffalo. At Buffalo on July 3, 1832, Gatlin and his classmates boarded the steamer *Henry Clay* with General Scott, Major David Twiggs, three companies of artillery and three companies of Fourth Infantry and set out for war. Gatlin wrote of the situation, "Arriving in New York in June '32 when Genl Scott was about to set out, to take command in the Black Hawk War. We volunteered to accompany the troops destined for that war."[21]

After two days on Lake Erie, about one-third of the way to Chicago, the *Henry Clay* met trouble. Two men on board were dead when it steamed into Detroit. Asiatic cholera, a dread disease that had been lurking in isolated cases in Canada and along the northern border for some months, suddenly and fatally struck Winfield Scott's fleet. Scott transferred himself, his staff, the West Pointers and uninfected troops to the *Sheldon Thompson*, which had arrived at Detroit shortly after the *Henry Clay*, and steamed on. So many of the men were so violently sick by the time they reached Fort Gratiot, forty miles north of Detroit, that the *Henry Clay* and the *Superior* could go no farther. At Fort Gratiot, the troops disembarked helter-skelter in a mad rush to escape the deadly scourge. Many deserted, disappearing into the landscape, where they died painfully and alone. When order finally prevailed, Scott established a camp away from the fort. Gatlin greatly understated the situation when he wrote: "On arriving at Fort Gratiot the troops were landed from the Steamer *Henry Clay* (on which they had embarked at Buffalo on the 3rd July) in consequence of the cholera which prevailed to an alarming extent. The camp was pitched ½ mile below the fort."[22]

Aboard the other ships, the story was much the same—troops and crew were sick and dying. After depositing the West Pointers at the camp below Fort Gratiot, Scott directed the *Sheldon Thompson*, with himself on board, to proceed to Fort Dearborn accompanied by the *William Penn*, but he could not outrun the disease. Scott lost nearly half his 850-man force to death and desertion. After a week at Fort Gratiot, it became evident that to continue the *Henry Clay*'s voyage to Fort Dearborn would be fruitless, and Major Twiggs ordered the West Pointers to return to New York.[23]

The *Henry Clay*, with the West Pointers aboard, and the *Superior* returned to Buffalo. Thus, Gatlin's first foray into battle ended. He apparently did not contract cholera or suffer any symptoms. He was one of the lucky ones to survive. As devastating as the outbreak was, only five men actually died while on board the *Henry Clay*, although many more died after leaving the ship. The only one of the new brevet second lieutenants from West Point who did not make the return voyage to New York was twenty-two-year-old Franklin McDuffie, who remained at Fort Gratiot and succumbed to cholera on July 15, just fifteen days after graduating eleventh in the class of '32. From Buffalo, the surviving graduates struck out for their respective homes before reporting to their permanent duty stations. They had not experienced the trial of combat, but they did get an early, firsthand taste of the army's greatest foe—disease—the silent hand of death that was its mightiest enemy.

Scott's fatal expedition ultimately proved unnecessary, because a few weeks later, before Scott reached the fighting, the army gunboat *Warrior* surprised

A portrait of Mac-cut-i-mish-e-ca-cu-cac, or Black Hawk, painted by J.O. Lewis in 1833. *Library of Congress.*

and nearly annihilated Black Hawk and his band as they slipped across the Mississippi River. Black Hawk escaped but soon turned himself in. Second Lieutenant Jefferson Davis led the detachment that escorted Black Hawk to confinement at Jefferson Barracks, Missouri. With the Indian leader in captivity, the Black Hawk War ended.

With his volunteer stint in the Black Hawk War abruptly terminated, Richard Gatlin traveled home. He arrived in Kinston in late July, his first time home in more than four years, and reunited with his parents, sisters and elder brother, John Slade Gatlin, who had recently begun studying medicine, possibly under the direction of local physician Reuben Knox.

If Richard had a romantic interest in Kinston or elsewhere at this time, history is silent about it. Richard—slender, over six feet tall, hazel-eyed and with a full head of wavy, dark brown hair and a full set of muttonchop sideburns—was a striking figure. He apparently shied away from any serious relationships in this period of his life, possibly because brevet second lieutenants earned very little pay, hardly enough to support a family.

Richard joined the rolls of the Seventh U.S. Infantry effective August 24, 1832, with orders to report on November 1 to that regiment's headquarters at Fort Gibson, Indian Territory. When the nights began to cool in Kinston in mid-October, Brevet Second Lieutenant Richard Gatlin departed for Indian Territory.[21]

Chapter 4

"Charnel House of the Army": On the Indian Frontier

Long before the Indian Removal Act became law in 1830, the American government had persuaded some southeastern Indians to vacate their lands and move to the West. In 1814, nearly two thousand Cherokees migrated from Georgia to a large tract of land, granted them by the United States, between the Arkansas and White Rivers, in the Missouri Territory. Some of the Cherokees crossed onto Osage land, and a portion of the Cherokee claim was in lands hunted by the Osage. Thus, trouble between the Cherokee and Osage quickly developed and continued to fester. In 1817, the United States made another treaty with the eastern Cherokees, granting them a tract of land encompassing most of today's northern Arkansas in exchange for a like amount of eastern Cherokee land. Cherokees began streaming westward, and open warfare developed between the Osage and the western Cherokees. To control the situation in the West, the government established a small army post in present-day Arkansas, on the Osage/Cherokee border at a place called Belle Point where the Poteau River enters the Arkansas River. They named it Fort Smith. Unfortunately, the fort proved to be too far east and too undermanned to influence the Cherokee and Osage to make peace, so in 1824, the army directed the troops at Fort Smith to establish a new post farther upriver, deeper into Creek territory. Colonel Matthew Arbuckle, longtime army officer and commander of the Seventh U.S. Infantry at Fort Smith, led a small contingent of soldiers up the Arkansas River to the mouth of the Verdigris River (near present-day Tahlaquah, Oklahoma) and established Cantonment Gibson.[25]

Missionaries and traders had been in the area since 1820 and had crisscrossed the Cantonment Gibson site for several years. However, the coming of an army post opened the way for a far greater white presence. Almost immediately after Cantonment Gibson's appearance, steamboats began plying their way to the post, farther up the Arkansas than had been thought possible. Within three years, the army had built a road from Little Rock to Cantonment Gibson and all but abandoned Fort Smith. Built of green logs and located in a low, swampy area, Cantonment Gibson, called the "charnel house of the army" by its unfortunate garrison, was a miserable, malarial place in constant need of repair. Scores of soldiers became sick and died from the "miasma" associated with the area, but the post was strategically located and was probably the most important of the frontier forts of its era. The fort's presence quelled the simmering hostility among the area tribes, deterred white traders from selling liquor to the Indians and offered migrating Indians a place of respite before embarking on the journey to their new homelands to the west. By 1832, Cantonment Gibson had been renamed Fort Gibson, but it was still well outside the limits of civilization and on the edge of the American frontier. The fort's mission had changed somewhat since its establishment. It was rapidly becoming the terminus for Indians migrating westward from their Georgia, Florida, Alabama, Mississippi and Tennessee homelands.[26]

Elements of the Seventh Infantry had garrisoned the cantonment from its founding, but in 1832, Fort Gibson became the official home to all ten companies of the Seventh Infantry.[27] The infantry's responsibility was to escort the migrating Indians from the east to Fort Gibson and from Fort Gibson to their new homes in Indian Territory. An infantry regiment included a colonel, who commanded the regiment; a lieutenant colonel; a major; one or two surgeons; and ten companies of soldiers. Each company consisted of a captain, who commanded the company; a first lieutenant; a second lieutenant; sometimes a brevet second lieutenant; and about forty-five enlisted men. Thus, some five hundred soldiers were at Fort Gibson in 1832, along with a number of wives, laundresses, the sutler and his family and a few assorted others. Companies carried the designating letters "A" through "I" and the letter "K." The letter "J" was excluded because it looked too much like "I" when written.[28]

Embarking by stagecoach from Kinston in mid-October 1832, Gatlin journeyed for two months, exploring his way west via Knoxville, Nashville and Memphis. He arrived at Fort Gibson on December 10, 1832, and reported to Colonel Arbuckle, who still commanded both the post and the

Seventh Infantry. Then, assigned to Company H, he met his acting company commander, First Lieutenant Stephen W. Moore. Moore led him to his new home, a roughly constructed boarded shelter that passed for officers' quarters. Shabby quarters were a hallmark of Fort Gibson then and for years to come.[29]

Fewer than half of the fort's officers were present for duty when Gatlin arrived. Colonel Arbuckle and Major Sullivan Burbank were at the post along with only three of the ten captains, one of the ten first lieutenants and only two of the ten second lieutenants. The remaining officers were on detached service elsewhere, on furlough or were AWOL. Five of nine brevet second lieutenants, including Gatlin, were on hand.[30] Of the soldiers on the Seventh Infantry rolls in December 1832, many became Gatlin's closest friends and companions in the following years. The names of Dixon S. Miles, Benjamin Bonneville, T.H. Holmes, Washington Seawell, Francis Lee, Gabriel J. Rains, Edgar S. Hawkins, Stephen W. Moore, Richard H. Ross and Daniel P. Whiting eventually accompanied Gatlin's life. For now, though, the young lieutenant from Lenoir County was perhaps a little bewildered at the absence of so many officers at once. He was probably somewhat awed, too, by the barrenness of the Indian Territory and the dilapidation of the quarters at Fort Gibson. If things did not quite measure up to his expectations, however, he neither complained nor mentioned it in his writings.

In 1832, officers provided their own weapons, and Gatlin undoubtedly had brought from home his personal pistol outfitted with the recently invented percussion cap device that had not yet replaced the flintlock on army-issued small arms. A week after his arrival, on December 17, while standing his first guard duty, Gatlin fired a weapon, possibly his new pistol, but the percussion cap exploded back toward him, launching a metal shard into his left eye, blinding him. When the post surgeon was unable to remove the metal piece from Gatlin's eye, Colonel Arbuckle ordered Gatlin to New Orleans for treatment.

On January 10, 1833, the wounded Lieutenant Gatlin departed Fort Gibson, boated down the Arkansas River to the Mississippi River and, within days, steamed into the Crescent City. This was his first of many experiences on the mighty Mississippi, but he laconically omitted any reference to it in his writings. Once in New Orleans, Gatlin sought out army surgeon Thomas Lawson, later to be United States surgeon general. Lawson tried minor surgery but was unable to extract the implanted metal and recommended that Gatlin take medical leave. The discouraged young Gatlin, following a two-month stay in New Orleans, opted to return home to Kinston. He wrote to the army's adjutant general on March 7, 1833:

> *Being advised by Doctor Lawson to visit my native clime and spend a short time for the benefit of one of my eyes, which received a very severe injury at Fort Gibson some time in Decr. last, and which is now in such a state, that to extract the foreign body from it, would endanger the loss, not only of the sight, but of the ball itself; and believing that should I now return to my post, I should not be fit for military duty for many months to come: I am induced to apply for an extension of my furlough, for the purpose of visiting my parents, at Kinston No Carolina, there to remain until nature shall have given me relief or in case it should become necessary to go to Philadelphia and obtain the advice of Doctor Phisioc as to the propriety of operating.*
>
> *You will find here with enclosed, the certificate of Doctor Lawson—together with the furlough granted me by Col. Arbuckle which authorizes me to apply for this extension and by virtue of which I am now absent from Fort Gibson.*
>
> *You will please direct your communications to me on the subject, at Kinston, No Carolina as I shall leave for that place in a few days.*[31]

Gatlin sailed on March 13 aboard the brig *Leo* to Baltimore, probably sailed down the Chesapeake Bay to Norfolk and then took a stagecoach to Kinston.[32]

Passing the summer of 1833 in Kinston had little curative effect on Gatlin's eye. However, by September 15, 1833, the inflammation had at least subsided, so against his doctor's protests, Gatlin once again set out for Fort Gibson. He made the long, arduous journey by stage to Memphis and then by horseback across Missouri and Arkansas. On October 30, 1833, Gatlin arrived again at Fort Gibson, where, although he had virtually no army experience, he defaulted to command of Company E, his first command.

It was common for a low-ranking officer like Gatlin to assume temporary command of a company in the absence of any higher-ranking officers. In this case, the regular company commander, Captain/Brevet Major George Birch, was on furlough, and the other lieutenants in the company were away on extra duty assignments, so Gatlin was the only officer available to command the company. On January 4, 1834, Dragoon Major Richard B. Mason chose Gatlin's Company E to accompany his mounted troops for a foray into Indian Territory to, as Gatlin said, "drive Osage Indians off the Creek lands."[33] Gatlin wrote of the expedition: "The weather had been extremely cold so that we crossed the Verdigris River twice on the ice. It

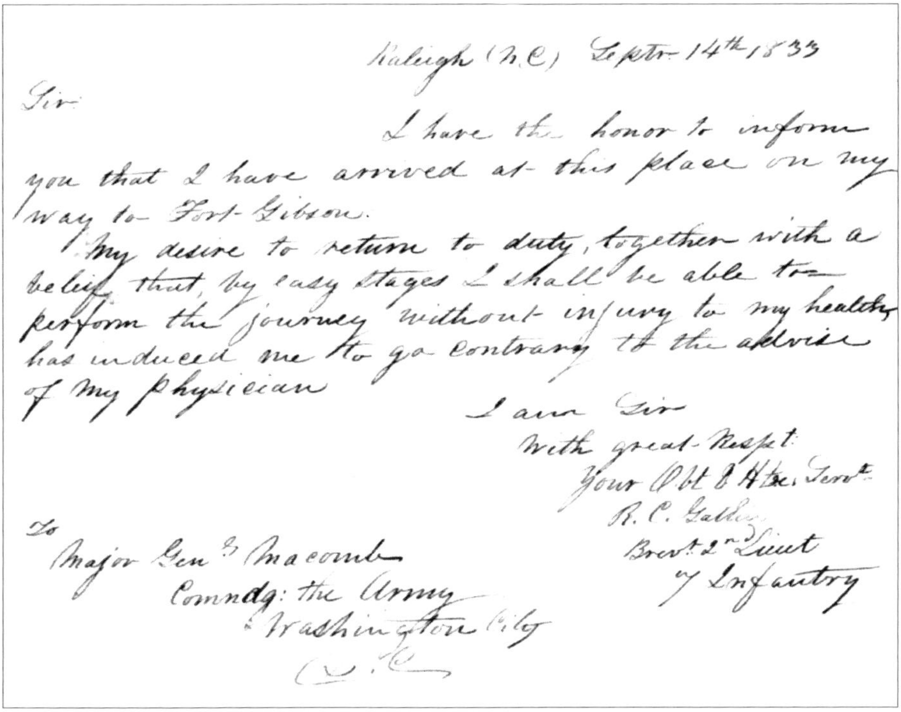

Raleigh (N.C) Septr 14th 1833

Sir

I have the honor to inform you that I have arrived at this place on my way to Fort Gibson.

My desire to return to duty, together with a belief that, by easy stages I shall be able to perform the journey without injury to my health has induced me to go contrary to the advice of my physician

I am Sir
With great Respect
Your Obt & Hble. Servt.
R. C. Gatlin
Brevt 2d Lieut
7 Infantry

To
Major Genl. Macomb
Comndg: the Army
Washington City

Gatlin's letter to Major General Alexander Macomb concerning his eye injury. *Taken from* Letters Received by the Adjutant General, 1822–1860 *via Fold3.*

had been thick enough to bear a wagon and team. Thermometer had been as low as 7° below zero. Returned after an absence of eight days having accomplished the object of this expedition."[34]

This was Gatlin's first experience commanding troops in the field, so he undoubtedly followed Major Mason's example closely. Mason was a Virginian, the grandson of George Mason, who was the "Father of the Bill of Rights." Proud and seasoned, Mason was a stern, no-nonsense type of officer who would later become military governor of California Territory during the gold rush era. In the fall of 1833, Mason arrived at Fort Gibson with the first contingent of the newly organized First Dragoons, a precursor to the cavalry. The remainder of the dragoons reached Fort Gibson from Jefferson Barracks, Missouri, in June 1834. Their mission was to march, in a show of strength, to the outer limits of Indian Territory to compel the plains tribes to treat with the federal government. Brigadier General Henry Leavenworth commanded the dragoons, Colonel Henry Dodge was his subordinate and Major Mason was third in command. Among the other officers were Captain Nathan Boone, son of pioneer Daniel Boone, and First Lieutenant Jefferson Davis.[35]

In preparation for the Dragoon Expedition, Companies I and K of the Seventh Infantry, under command of First Lieutenant Stephen W. Moore, began building a road from Fort Gibson southward about 125 miles across the Canadian River to the mouth of the False Washita River. Gatlin transferred to and took command of Company I on May 7, 1834, and caught up with Moore's battalion that had left Fort Gibson two days earlier. Gatlin wrote of this assignment:

> *On this route no Indians were settled west of the North Fork of the Canadian, crossed the Canadian at the mouth of Little River, found buffalo ten miles from the crossing. They were abundant on the Boggy and Blue Water near which stream we found a band of Osages making their summer's hunt. Finished the road on the 16th of June, and set out for Gibson.*[36]

While on this excursion, Gatlin received his first promotion, to full second lieutenant, on May 30, 1834.[37]

During the return march to Fort Gibson, Gatlin encountered Second Lieutenant Theophilus H. Holmes, and Company B of the Seventh Infantry busily engaged in building a small fort along the new road where it crossed the Canadian River near the mouth of the Little River. Holmes and Gatlin were well acquainted even before Gatlin had arrived at Fort Gibson, having been from nearby counties in North Carolina and having been fellow cadets at West Point. Holmes had orders for Gatlin and his company to remain and help build the new fort, which they named Camp Holmes. For two long, blistering months, the companies labored together until finally both Holmes and Gatlin were too sick from fever—likely malaria, which was common around the swampy western forts—to advance any farther. First Lieutenant Washington Seawell arrived from Fort Gibson on September 9 to take command of the battalion and lead it back to Fort Gibson. Gatlin found himself on the "sick" roll from September through October 1834, and Holmes remained sick one month longer than that. Gatlin described the experience thusly:

> *On arriving at the Canadian on the 22nd found Lt Holmes with B Co. with orders to detain I Co. to assist in building a fort at that point. Commenced work and labored hard until the 1st Septr when orders were received to abandon the post and return to Gibson, but had to wait for an offr. (Lt*

> *Seawell) to conduct the command—Holmes and myself being too sick to undertake it. Left on the 9th and arrived at Fort Gibson 15 Septr/34.*[38]

Meanwhile, in mid-June 1834, the Leavenworth-Dodge Dragoon Expedition got underway with over 500 men, including a number of civilian observers, notably author Washington Irving and artist George Catlin. The expedition departed with high expectations that soon evaporated with the blazing plains sun and a shortage of water. Troopers fell by the wayside in clusters with fever and dysentery, and many died on the trail. General Leavenworth fell from his horse while chasing a buffalo, lingered for several days and then died on July 21. Only a small, pitiable contingent headed by Colonel Dodge and Major Mason finally reached the Comanche and Kiowa camps before beginning a long retreat to Fort Gibson in August 1834.[39] By the time the expeditionary force arrived at Fort Gibson, more than 150 troopers were dead, and many more suffered debilitating illnesses.

Artist and ethnographer George Catlin, whose paintings remain some of today's best glimpses into the American past, had traveled from Philadelphia to accompany the expedition, intending to document life among the plains Indians. But Catlin nearly paid for the

Dragoons Crossing the Canadian River in Indian Territory in 1834. Painting by George Catlin. *Smithsonian Museum of Art.*

A miniature of R.C. Gatlin probably painted by George Catlin, circa 1834. *North Carolina Museum of History*.

experience with his own life.[10] Although he survived the trek, he was very sick for weeks, teetering on the brink of death at one point. Following the expedition, during the time that Catlin and Gatlin were both at Fort Gibson, Catlin painted a miniature oval portrait of Lieutenant Gatlin that later became a prized possession of Gatlin's youngest daughter until she donated it to the North Carolina Museum of History in 1968.

During the ensuing eighteen months, Gatlin remained in garrison at Fort Gibson, occasionally accompanying expeditions into the Indian Territory but generally involving himself with temporary company command and administrative chores such as court-martial duty. Day in and day out, the officers and men experienced the monotony of army life. The morning bugle roused the troops from bed at daybreak, and the resounding boom of the morning gun ensured that no one slept in. Following a flag-raising ceremony, work details went about the business of gardening, feeding and watering the livestock, repairing buildings, cleaning weapons and drilling, drilling, drilling. The officers drilled the newer recruits incessantly to the chagrin—but also the benefit—of all.

Indians and traders, including the fort's sutlers, Robert Stuart Gibson and widow Sallie Nicks, were constantly about the fort providing a welcome diversion. Along with playing cards, knives, combs, tobacco and the myriad and sundry items so treasured by the troops, traders brought news of happenings in the East and elsewhere. The garrison eagerly greeted new arrivals by land and by the occasional steamboat that made it up the Arkansas River in periods of high water. Especially welcome were the young women who ventured from the East to this wilderness oasis, sometimes in hopes of just meeting the gallant young officers and men of the Seventh Infantry and First Dragoons, and sometimes in hopes of marrying one of them. The several weddings that took place at Fort Gibson were always major social events. Despite the frequent visits by white women, many more soldiers than women occupied Fort Gibson, and the men often sought the company of local Cherokee and part-Cherokee girls from the surrounding reservation. Officers, too, occasionally cavorted with the females of the reservation. Not all of the fort's social gatherings were joyous occasions, however. Too frequently, the harsh and unhealthy conditions at the fort were responsible for a more somber type of social event: funerals.

The monotony broke at least briefly in December 1834, when, in the dragoon camp outside Fort Gibson, Major Mason arrested First Lieutenant Jefferson Davis for failing to report during morning roll call. Davis had remained in his tent during the rainy morning, which he felt was within army regulations. Rightly or wrongly, Mason required all officers to attend roll call regardless of weather. When Mason confronted him, Davis contemptuously turned and walked away, muttering something incoherent and refusing to acknowledge any wrongdoing. Because of that clear act of insubordination, Mason preferred charges against Davis, and a court-martial convened at Fort Gibson in February 1835. Arbuckle, Gatlin, Holmes and several other officers of the Seventh Infantry sat on the jury. After days of deliberations, Gatlin and the jury proclaimed Davis "guilty of the specifications exhibited against him" but noted that his actions as contained in the specifications were devoid of any criminality. Consequently, the jury acquitted Davis of the charges.[11] Less than three weeks later, on March 2, 1835, Davis handed General Arbuckle a letter of resignation and departed for a forty-day furlough to Kentucky to marry Sarah Knox Taylor, the daughter of Colonel Zachary Taylor. When Davis did not return to Fort Gibson after forty days, Arbuckle submitted the resignation to the War Department, and Jefferson Davis, future Confederate president, was out of the army effective June 30, 1835. Davis and his new bride settled at Brierfield, a Mississippi plantation given them by his brother, but both newlyweds fell ill, and the young Mrs. Davis died on September 15, 1835.[12]

At Fort Gibson, the spring and summer of 1835 offered little significant diversion from the normal tedium of garrison life. The hot and humid weather was abysmal. Sickness prevailed at the "sinkhole" of the army, so every week another detachment escaped the fort and headed into the prairie, partly to get relief from the heat and "miasma" and partly to seek out illicit whiskey and to chase any white men who brought it in. Captain Francis Lee took two companies south to the False Washita looking for whiskey, Lieutenant Francis Page and a small detachment did the same closer to Fort Gibson and in April 1835, Lieutenant Gatlin led a ten-man detachment escorting "villainous" white men out of the territory.[13] In May 1835, Major Mason led a summer expedition 150 miles to the southwest of Fort Gibson and established an encampment. His purpose was to meet with the western Indians—Comanche, Osage and Kiowa in particular—to establish "amicable relations" along the Texas border, but as with the Leavenworth expedition the year before, many of the troopers fell ill. In June, Second Lieutenant Augustine Seaton, who had traveled west with artist George Catlin to Fort Gibson the previous year, led a thirty-man supply battalion to the relief of Mason, but while returning to Fort Gibson in July, Seaton was stranded at the Little River for eleven days by unrelenting rains. The extended cold and wet had its effect on Seaton, who was gravely ill by the time he and his detachment staggered back into Fort Gibson. The twenty-five-year-old lieutenant lingered but died at Fort Gibson on November 25, 1835.[14]

Meanwhile, Richard Gatlin's elder brother, John Slade Gatlin, now twenty-eight, had completed his medical study and had applied for a post as an assistant surgeon with the United States Army. In August 1834, having passed the required medical exams, Dr. John Gatlin was commissioned into the army and assigned to his brother's regiment, the Seventh Infantry. Leaving Kinston in August, plying the Atlantic Ocean to Key West, crossing the Gulf of Mexico to New Orleans, then steaming up the Mississippi and Arkansas Rivers and finally traveling by horseback into the Indian Territory, John joined Richard on November 6, 1834, at Fort Gibson. Their reunion was short-lived, however, for orders were waiting for Dr. Gatlin to report to Camp Arbuckle, a temporary and lonely outpost deep in Indian Territory fifty miles northwest of Fort Gibson.[45] Bidding Richard a quick adieu, John set out to join the seventy-five men of Company E who had been detached from Fort Gibson to build and garrison Camp Arbuckle that summer.

Having grown up among the genteel people of Kinston and eastern North Carolina, John found the wild desolation of Camp Arbuckle maddening. Much to his relief, though, only three months after his arrival, Company E abandoned Camp Arbuckle and returned to Fort Gibson, where the Gatlin brothers reunited in February 1835. This family reunion was also short-lived, however, because even though his career had been brief, young Dr. Gatlin was not of a nature to spend any more of it away from society than necessary. The isolation at Camp Arbuckle had convinced him to apply for a better assignment back east, and he was excited to learn on arriving at Fort Gibson that the army had approved it. The Gatlin brothers passed less than a month together at Fort Gibson, and then John left by steamboat, en route by way of Fort Jackson, Louisiana, to a new duty station in Pensacola, Florida.[46] In late March 1835, he settled in at Fort Pickens with a small detachment of the Second Artillery in company with Captain George W. Gardiner and First Lieutenant William Basinger. A steamy, lonely summer in Pensacola did not suit Dr. Gatlin either, but his sinking spirits rose when he learned that autumn of the reassignment of the Fort Pickens detachment, including Captain Gardiner, Lieutenant Basinger and himself, to Tampa Bay. The army in late 1835 had begun channeling its force into central Florida, where the Seminole Indians were resisting relocation to the West. In late December 1835, Dr. John Gatlin and his Second Artillery companions steamed across the Gulf of Mexico and debarked at Fort Brooke at Tampa Bay, Florida Territory.

The Seminoles were openly hostile to United States efforts to relocate them westward to Indian Territory, partly because they feared the government would rob them of their slaves.[47] The U.S. government and Andrew Jackson had waged the First Seminole War in 1818, primarily to open Florida to American settlement but also to recapture runaway slaves who had crossed the Florida border and taken up with the local Indians. Despite Jackson's successes, however, slaves continued to escape from the Deep South into Florida, where they assimilated into the Seminole bands, usually remaining as Seminole slaves but with a degree of freedom unknown to them in the slave states. In addition, Seminoles often raided white-owned Florida plantations and stole slaves for their own.[48] Targeted by the Indian

Removal Act of 1830 and having signed a questionable 1833 agreement to leave Florida, the Seminoles faced a dilemma: go to a faraway land much drier and colder than Florida and risk losing their slaves or fight any efforts to remove them.

Ultimately, the recalcitrant Indians struck. On December 28, 1835, a Seminole band under the warrior Osceola surprised and killed the Indian agent and others at Fort King in north-central Florida. Almost simultaneously, a war party of Seminoles and blacks, under Chiefs Micanopy and Alligator, ambushed Major Francis Dade's 108-man detachment, then en route from Fort Brooke to Fort King, killing Dade and 105 others, including Captain Gardiner and Lieutenant Basinger, the newly arrived transfers from Fort Pickens. Among the last of the detachment to be slain was the assistant surgeon who had just recently arrived in Florida with Gardiner and Basinger, Dr. John Slade Gatlin, who, with two double-barreled shotguns in hand, was said to have challenged the attackers with the cry, "I've got four of 'em for you!"[49] The attackers left the dead men to the ravages of nature where they lay. During the next several months, Seminoles and blacks wreaked havoc in Florida. To the plantation owners in Florida and other southern states, Florida Territory was in the midst of a slave revolt. To the United States government, the long and expensive Second Seminole War had begun.[50]

Lieutenant Richard Gatlin probably did not learn of his brother's death until some weeks after it had occurred. If he had designs on returning to Kinston to comfort his family, he did not act on them because events were heating up on the Southwestern Plains as well as in Florida.

In early 1836, the people of Texas, then part of the Mexican state of Coahuila y Tejas, were in revolt against the Mexican government.[51] Sam Houston, a former Tennessee governor, had passed through Fort Gibson in 1831 and had at one time hoped to become the fort's sutler. Now, Houston was the commander of the so-called Texas Army. In February 1836, volunteers from Tennessee, led by legendary former congressional representative Davy Crockett, passed through Arkansas on their way to join the Texas revolt. On March 2, 1836, Texas declared its independence, and the United States Army stood poised to watch carefully the unfolding drama. Word arrived at Fort Gibson that the Mexican army under Generalissimo Antonio Lopez de Santa Anna had annihilated the 180-man corps of defenders under Colonel William Travis at the Alamo in San Antonio and had summarily executed 342 Texas defenders under Colonel James Fannin at Goliad. In the aftermath of those infamous disasters, the Texan revolutionaries won their

Massacre of Major Dade and His Command. This engraving, published in 1847 in Barber's *Incidents in American History*, depicts Hitchcock's discovery of the Dade battleground. *Wikimedia Commons.*

independence by surprising and smashing the army of Santa Anna at the Battle of San Jacinto in April 1836.

Although he surrendered and agreed to the Texans' demands for independence, Santa Anna's continued presence in Mexico threatened an uneasy peace. The specter of a Mexican resurgence and rumors that the Plains Indians might begin raiding northern Texas persisted. General Edmund Gaines, commander of the American army of the West, thus ordered the Seventh Infantry from Fort Gibson to the Texas border town of Nacogdoches to serve as a buffer between the Texans and the Indians. Departing in early May under command of Lieutenant Colonel William Whistler, Gatlin and six companies of the Seventh Infantry marched southward to Fort Towson. In July, the battalion proceeded to Nacogdoches, just inside the Texas border, where they remained for five months until it was clear that the Indians intended no hostility to the Texans or to the United States.[52] On August 30, 1836, while in Nacogdoches, twenty-seven-year-old Gatlin accepted a promotion to first lieutenant. Gatlin tersely wrote of this entire experience:

> *Left Gibson on 5th May/36 with a detachment of six companies under Lt Col Whistler for Fort Towson to watch the course of events in Texas.*

Log commanding officer's quarters at Fort Gibson. *Photo by John Stanton.*

> *Arrived at Towson 17th May. Left Towson July 15th for Nacogdoches, Texas and arrived there 30th. Remained in Nacogdoches until 15th Decr. when I was ordered to proceed on the return route as far as the Sabine and there prepare a means of crossing. The Command constructed a couple of canoes and fastened them five ½ ft. apart, layed* [sic] *a platform of split pine wood across them and thus enabled the train to pass the river with as much ease as in an ordinary Ferry fleet. Crossed on the 24th and was joined by the command on that day. Arrived at Fort Gibson on 15th January 1837. Distance from Nacogdoches 400 miles, all of which I marched save for about 11 miles when unwell.*[53]

During Gatlin's sojourn at Fort Towson, his father, who was despondent over the death of his elder son, died in Kinston on June 20, 1836. John Gatlin was buried at the Caswell Family Cemetery at the Red House Plantation near Kinston.[54] Though it must have grieved Gatlin to lose both his brother and father in so short a time, he nonetheless remained with his command rather than requesting a furlough. Finally, when the Seventh Infantry returned to Fort Gibson in January 1837, and with the threat of an Indian uprising ended, Gatlin turned his attention to his remaining family. He requested a furlough and learned of his reassignment to the East. Following more than three full years in Indian Territory, Richard Gatlin started for home.

Chapter 5

"Remember the *Caroline*": The Patriot's War

During Gatlin's three-year stay in Indian Territory, North Carolina had experienced an awakening of sorts. For the first one-third of the nineteenth century, North Carolina had progressed so little socially and economically that it earned the nickname "Rip Van Winkle State" after Washington Irving's fictional character who slept for twenty years. Now, during a new era of awakening, "the broad middle eastern section," including Kinston, "was the most attractive, wealthy, developed, and cultured area in North Carolina," according to historians Hugh Lefler and Albert Newsom.[55]

The "Jacksonian Era," initiated by the 1828 election of Andrew Jackson to the presidency, changed much of American government, politics, education, finance, business, transportation, expansion and social discourse. Jackson's administration appealed to great masses of farmers and workers, and his general influence waned little until the Civil War tore the country apart more than three decades later. His Democratic Republican Party viewed the United States as a confederation of states with only limited national authority and influence. This served Jackson well at first, but by opposing federal expenditures for local internal improvements and by approving appointments of friends and supporters to federal office, he began to disappoint various regional people of influence. In 1832, South Carolina's Ordinance of Nullification protested that the federal trade tariff favored northern manufacturers to the agricultural South's detriment, was unconstitutional and was inapplicable to South Carolina. Jackson declared, ironically, that no state had the right to rule any federal law null and void, nor had the right to leave the Union; thus, Jackson alienated much of the rural South and West. Jackson's response to nullification forced the hand of Vice President John C. Calhoun of South Carolina, who broke openly with Jackson and resigned his office. This national philosophical schism resulted in the establishment in 1834 of the Whig Party, organized by many of the country's ablest and learned men, men such as former president John Quincy Adams, Senator Henry Clay from Kentucky and Daniel Webster of Massachusetts. Significantly, many westerners who had formerly supported Jackson now joined the Whigs. Spurred by a new group of Whig leaders, mostly from west of Raleigh, change accelerated in the Old North State. Nationalist-leaning North Carolinians such as David L. Swain of Buncombe County, Edward Dudley of Wilmington and John M. Morehead of Guilford County, all of whom became governors, joined the Whig Party. In fact, Whigs dominated North Carolina politics during most of the 1830s and 1840s.

The events of the early 1830s began to stir the state from its slumber. Another phenomenon completed the awakening, as the emergence of railroad technology promised to resolve North Carolina's transportation dilemma. With the Whigs came a new impetus for internal improvements in North Carolina, especially in transportation. Railroads were just coming into existence in other parts of the country, and at Whig urging, a private group obtained a charter for the Wilmington & Weldon Railroad in North Carolina in 1834. In 1835, another group chartered the Raleigh and Gaston Railroad. The state granted the railroads financial aid, and railroad building got underway. When the completion of both railroads in 1840 linked eastern North Carolina to markets in Virginia, people across the entire state began clamoring for railways. By the late 1830s, North Carolina was well on the way to becoming one of the most progressive states of the South.

Another effect of the emergence of the Whig Party in North Carolina was that the political dominance of the eastern part of the state was broken. Eastern and western North Carolina were becoming more similar anyway, thanks in part to a shared resentment of the growing abolitionist movement and to the increasing size of western farms due to the rise of tobacco culture in the Piedmont. In 1835, the demand for governmental reform became so acute that North Carolina held a constitutional referendum. Under Whig influence, the state amended its constitution to eliminate the power lock that the landed gentry had held on state politics for nearly sixty years.

On January 29, 1837, in the cold of winter, Richard Gatlin left Fort Gibson and the frozen plains of Indian Territory for his home in North Carolina. Of this event, Gatlin wrote, "Left Fort Gibson on the 29th Jany '37 for North Carolina. My father had died in June '36 and it was important that I should return to look after my mother and sisters. Crossed the country on horseback to St Genevieve Mo. where took boat."[56]

Gatlin had not been home since departing Kinston for Fort Gibson in September 1833, nearly three and a half years earlier. Ice and low water in the Arkansas River probably prevented his taking a steamer or keelboat down to Fort Smith and then to the jumping-off point at Arkansas Post where the Arkansas River joined the Mississippi. He chose instead to trudge across the frosty Missouri hills alone on horseback as far as St. Genevieve, where he took a steamer down the Mississippi River to New Orleans. He then sailed around Florida, probably to Wilmington, North Carolina, or Charleston, South Carolina. Officially assigned to recruiting service on January 26, he needed to spend time on recruiting business in North Carolina. On April 6, 1837, he was in Fayetteville, North Carolina, to "close an indebtedness left open by Lt. Holmes for want of funds to pay expenses when he left in the previous winter."[57]

By April 26, 1837, Gatlin was in Wilmington to organize a group of North Carolina recruits and send them up the coast to their mustering point in Boston, Massachusetts. With that chore accomplished, he returned to Kinston and went on a well-deserved furlough that had officially begun on April 10, 1837.

When Gatlin reached North Carolina, it had been well over a year since the death of his brother, John Slade Gatlin, in Florida and ten months since his father's death in Kinston. Waiting for him were his mother, Susannah Gatlin, and sisters: Ann Lovick, Mary Gatlin and Catherine Reavis. Gatlin's youngest sister, Catherine, had married twenty-two-year-old Wake County lawyer Turner Reavis on January 20, 1835, in Kinston. Their first child, a boy named Richard Caswell Reavis, died during or shortly after his birth in 1836, around the same time that John Gatlin had died.

On May 30, 1837, in Kinston, Mary Gatlin, in her mid-twenties, wed a young physician, Dr. Franklin Knox. The Mary Gatlin–Franklin Knox marriage was the social event of the season in Kinston, but it must have been a bittersweet event for Susannah Gatlin, because shortly after their marriage, the newlyweds departed Kinston for a new home in bustling and growing St. Louis, Missouri. In St. Louis, Dr. Knox hoped to take advantage of the swelling westward-bound population and establish a thriving practice. Meanwhile, Gatlin's half sister, Ann Lovick, nearing forty, married the Reverend Curtis Hooks, a distant relative of Gatlin's friend T.H. Holmes. Reverend Hooks lived in Everettsville, near Goldsboro, in Wayne County, where, after their fall 1837 wedding, he took his new bride.

With her daughters Mary in St. Louis and Ann planning to live in Everettsville, Susannah Gatlin had little reason to remain in Kinston. Only Catherine lived nearby, and she and Turner Reavis were making plans to move to Alabama. Richard, of course, would soon be leaving for his next duty assignment. When Reverend Hooks and his new wife, Ann, proposed to Susannah Gatlin that she accompany them to Everettsville to live, Susannah readily accepted. Less than a year later, on March 24, 1838, Catherine Reavis died in a second childbirth and was buried at the Red House Cemetery.[58] The baby, a girl named Susan Gatlin Reavis, survived, but when Turner Reavis left Kinston in 1839 to set up law practice in Alabama and took his infant daughter with him, it marked the end of the Gatlin family in Kinston.

Richard Gatlin was well acquainted by this time with several former and future governors, senators and congressional representatives. Among these was his cousin by marriage, David L. Swain, North Carolina's governor from 1832 to 1835 and future president of the University of North Carolina. Another was future governor and Whig Party national vice presidential candidate William A. Graham of Hillsborough, whose wife was Eleanor White, a cousin and close friend of Gatlin's mother. Had he chosen to remain in Kinston, Gatlin might have retained and managed the family plantation and, with his connections, might have carved out a lucrative political career in his home state. However, at the tender age of twenty-eight, a more compelling force apparently drove him. Perhaps it was a sense of duty or perhaps a need to atone for his brother's death. Perhaps he was sobered or frightened by the economic depression of 1837. Perhaps it was simply the prospect of the steady pay and unending adventure offered by the army, for the U.S. frontier was bursting at the seams with expansion and growth in 1837. For whatever reason, Gatlin stayed the course he had set when he had entered West Point nine years before. Though some of his classmates had left the service already, First Lieutenant Gatlin chose to continue in the army.

Gatlin received orders, upon completion of his furlough, to report to the recruiting station at Brooklyn, New York. In late June 1837, he said his goodbyes, departed Kinston once again and headed north, arriving in Brooklyn on July 8. He began his recruiting assignment in earnest due to the desperate need for new troops for the ongoing Second Seminole War. In addition, and more significant to Gatlin at the time, trouble was brewing on the northern frontier that threatened to bring war between the United States and Great Britain.

In 1837, Canada was a British province with two political and geographic divisions. Lower Canada, at the eastern end of the St. Lawrence River, comprised the French-speaking regions of Montreal and Quebec. Upper Canada, farther west, near the upper end of the St. Lawrence River, included Ontario and Toronto and all points west. Some French-speaking Lower Canadians, protesting for Canadian separation from Great Britain, mounted a mild revolt in Quebec in the spring of 1837. The British deployed soldiers not only to Lower Canada to quell the movement but to Upper Canada as well.

Resentful of the British presence, several hundred English-speaking Canadian separatists threatened the arsenal at Toronto's city hall, but Loyalist militia fired on and dispersed them. Some escaped across Lake Ontario to Buffalo, New York, where they recruited some American sympathizers and formed the Patriot's army. On December 13, 1837, the Patriot's army, declaring to have established an independent nation, occupied Canada's tiny Navy Island in the Niagara River between Buffalo and Canada. Canadian militia colonel Allen McNab reacted to this declaration of independence by leading his militiamen across the Niagara River from Canada to Schlosser, New York, docking place of the American steamer *Caroline*. McNab recognized the *Caroline* as one of several ships used for transporting supplies from the United States to Patriots on Navy Island. McNab's men boarded the *Caroline*, loosed her moorings, set her afire and cast her adrift in the Niagara River, where she sank short of the Niagara Falls. In the mêlée, one man was killed, an American named Amos Durfee, but the rumor quickly spread that the burning ship had gone over the falls fully laden with terrified and screaming passengers and crew.

The *Caroline* affair sent instant shock waves throughout New York, the eastern United States and across the Great Lakes border with Canada, and it appeared that war between England and the United States might again be imminent. Just three days after the violent *Caroline* sinking, whether by design or happenstance, the army reassigned Lieutenant Gatlin from his recruiting station in Brooklyn to the military post at the state capital at Albany, New York. Gatlin reported in his journal, "After expiration of leave ordered on recruiting service and arrived in New York July 8 and was stationed in Brookline where I remained until the 22nd Decr. when I was ordered to Albany N.Y., where I relieved Maj Young on the 24th Decr/37."[59]

In Washington, within days, President Martin Van Buren dispatched the American army's second-ranking general, Winfield Scott, to the New York border with orders to smooth things over. The appearance of peacekeepers Scott and New York governor William L. Marcy in Buffalo helped quell the zeal of the Patriots, who, at Scott's urging, almost immediately disbanded.

That winter in early 1838, Gatlin recruited troops in nearby Albany, New York, for a newly authorized regular army regiment, the Eighth Infantry.

The peace that Scott had won along the Niagara was fraught with tension for months. It was suddenly shattered on the frigid night of May 30, 1838, when a vengeful remnant of the Patriot's army attacked and burned a peaceful civilian British passenger steamer. The *Sir Robert Peel*, with nineteen passengers aboard bound for Toronto, had stopped to take on wood when twenty-two marauders disguised as Indians swooped on board, shouting, "Remember the *Caroline*!" The passengers and crew were hustled ashore, leaving most of their baggage and personal belongings, and then the raiders set fire to the 130-foot steamer and shoved her into Lake Ontario to burn and sink. The acknowledged leader of the raiding party was forty-six-year-old Bill Johnston, a former grocery store owner from Lower Canada who had developed a revolutionary fervor against British Canadian rule during the War of 1812.

Governor Marcy quickly rose to the occasion and asked the U.S. secretary of war to mount an exhaustive effort to catch and punish the "pirates." In mid-June 1838, Major General Alexander Macomb, commanding general of the United States Army, dispatched Colonel William Jenkins Worth and elements of the new Eighth Infantry into the Thousand Islands, a broad stretch of the St. Lawrence River and Lake Ontario, aboard the steamer *Telegraph* to track down and apprehend Bill Johnston and his crew. Among Colonel Worth's subalterns was Lieutenant Gatlin, who led a company of new recruits on the mission. According to Gatlin:

> *Was relieved from Recruiting Service at Albany July 1, 1838 by Lt Myers, and ordered to Sackets Harbor where I arrived 3 July and was assigned to duty with a detachment of recruits. There was a considerable number of troops—mostly recruits assembled on the Northern Frontier at this time in consequence of the disturbances in Canada. Relieved Capt Gwynne 8th Inf in command of a Co. of recruits stationed on board the steamer* Telegraph *which cruises among the Thousand Islands and on the lake and river in search of the piratical crew, who had not long previous burned a British steamer, the* Sir Robert Peel, *on our side of the river, and to collect information of the movements of Patriots.*[60]

Despite extensively patrolling the boundary waters, the Eighth Infantry was unable to catch the elusive Bill Johnston and his henchmen. Colonel Worth found the pirates' retreat on a rocky little island known as the Devil's

A circa 1848 photo of General William J. Worth by Matthew B. Brady. *Wikimedia Commons*.

Oven but was unable to prevent Johnston's escape. Ultimately, the furor died down, summer ended and the *Telegraph*'s mission was discontinued.

The following summer, in June 1839, the army caught Bill Johnston and brought him to trial, but the jury acquitted him. Convicted of another offense soon afterward, Johnston escaped jail in 1841 and sneaked his way to Washington, D.C., where he managed to secure a pardon from President William Henry Harrison. Incredibly, the federal government then hired Johnston as a lighthouse keeper at Rock Island, New York, the very place where he had captured the *Sir Robert Peel*. He remained at that post for thirty years until his death in 1870.

On October 1, 1838, Gatlin was relieved of his special assignment aboard the *Telegraph*. With his pirate-chasing duties at an end, he went to Auburn, New York, to open a new recruiting rendezvous. Having efficiently taken care of that chore in under a month, he then received orders to leave New York and return to the Seventh Infantry headquarters at Fort Gibson. He would not be returning to Indian Territory as simply one of the subalterns (junior officers), however. He was the new regimental adjutant succeeding T.H. Holmes. The regimental adjutant was the administrative clerk for the regiment. His primary duties were to record regimental and personnel assignments and movements and to prepare regimental reports for submission to the adjutant general's office. Adjutancy was an honor usually reserved for the most thorough and conscientious of the regiment's lieutenants, so Gatlin

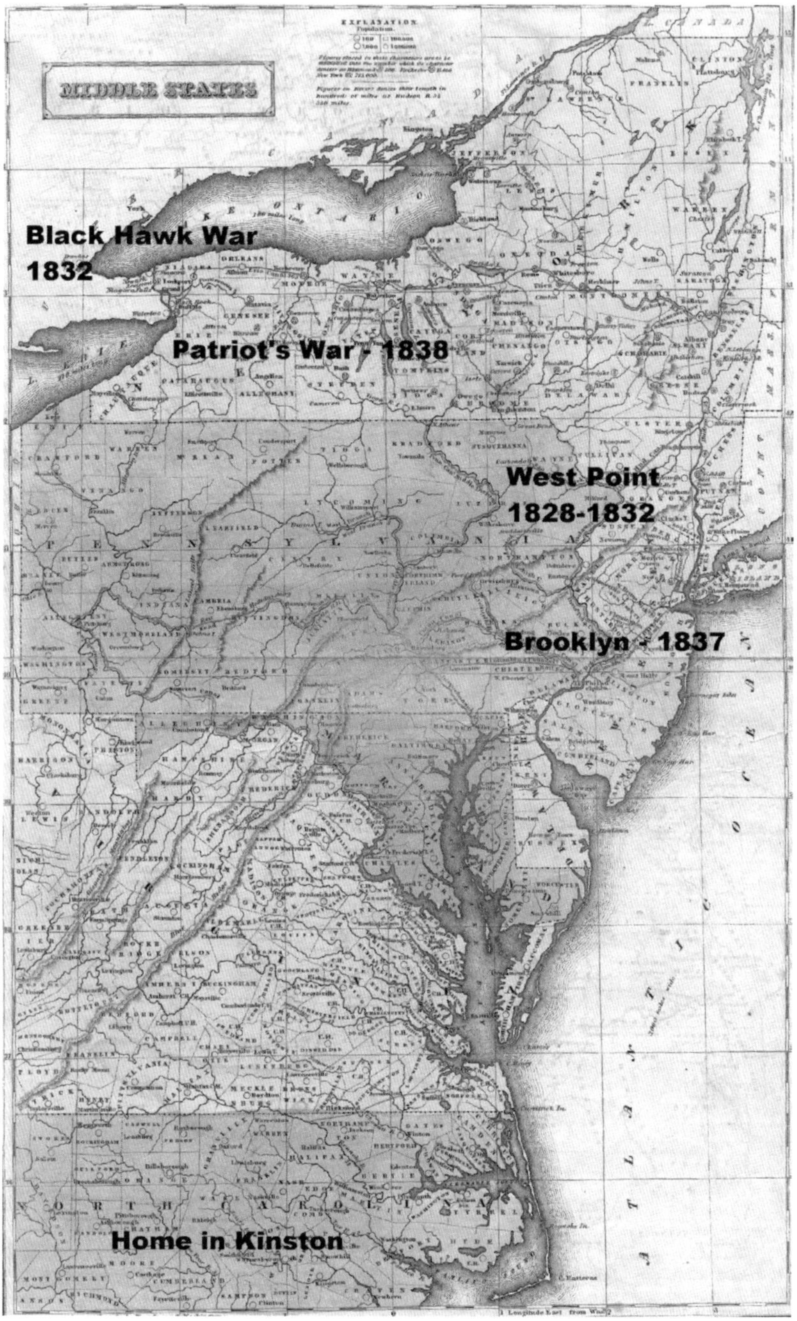

Gatlin's travels took him from Kinston to West Point, Lake Erie, Brooklyn and Upstate New York in the 1830s. *North Carolina Archives.*

must have impressed his superior officers with his administrative prowess. Gatlin, in his concise way, described the assignment thusly: "Was relieved from Recruiting Service Octr 31st and ordered to join my company at Fort Gibson. I proceeded by St Louis, thence to Jeff. City by stage and from thence on horseback to Fort Gibson where I arrived Decr. 20th/38. I found I had been appointed Adjutant of the 7th Inf. on the 13th Decr."[61]

Chapter 6

"I Did My Duty": The Seminole War

Upon arriving at Fort Gibson, Gatlin found more in store for him than simply assuming the adjutant's role. The entire Seventh Infantry, all ten companies, mustered at Fort Gibson for deployment to Florida. As soon as the men of the Fourth Infantry arrived from Florida to replace them at Fort Gibson, the Seventh Infantry sailed to Tampa Bay. General Arbuckle stayed on at Fort Smith as commander of the Second Military District, and Colonel William Whistler assumed command of Gatlin's regiment. Whistler had first joined the Seventh Infantry as a newly promoted lieutenant colonel on July 21, 1834, and, during his years as Arbuckle's fill-in commander at Fort Gibson, had become very popular with his troops.

The Second Seminole War was entering its fourth blood-filled year. What had begun with the slaughter of John Slade Gatlin and 105 other American soldiers at the Dade Massacre of December 1835 had evolved into a war of attrition and frustration for both the Seminoles and the American army. Despite having poured millions of dollars and thousands of men into the blistering Florida wilderness, the United States government had failed so far to relocate all the Seminoles from Florida to the Indian Territory.

The Seminoles were not indigenous to Florida. In fact, strictly speaking, they were not even a tribe. Rather, the Seminoles were an amalgamation of the remnants of several disappearing Florida tribes—Alachuas, Mikasukis, Tallahassees and others—disenfranchised Creeks who had been migrating southward from Georgia for nearly a century and runaway slaves. The British in Florida first used the term "Seminoles" to refer collectively to these diverse groups. Seminoles meant "wild ones," "separatists," "runaways" or words to that effect. It was convenient for the whites to use that one name for all the Florida Indians, regardless of the Indians' actual tribal affiliations.

In 1821, the United States purchased all of Florida from Spain. Removing the Seminoles became a goal of the new owners because it would open the territory to white farmers and ranchers, thus increasing land values and eliminating the safe harbor for runaway slaves. Seminoles presented a true danger to the white settlers, who, in turn, loudly vocalized their demands for Indian removal. Tensions and depredations between the newcomers and the Seminoles rose and fell regularly during the 1820s. A treaty drawn at Fort Moultrie near St. Augustine in 1823 restricted the Seminoles to an interior south-central Florida reservation, and it seemed for a while to be agreeable to both factions. However, Florida settlers could not remain comfortable as long as the Indians were in such close proximity. Then, the Indian Removal Act of 1830 formalized what had been the government's tacit policy of removing the Florida Indians to the Great Plains. By the Treaty of Payne's Landing, near present-day Gainesville, certain of the Seminoles promised in 1832 to take up lands in Indian Territory, west of Fort Gibson. Unfortunately, Creeks already occupied the lands, and the Seminoles balked at sharing a new home with their traditional enemies. Finally, on March 28, 1833, about the time Gatlin left New Orleans for Kinston to recover from his eye injury, a small group of Seminole chiefs met at Fort Gibson and agreed to resettle their people to a specified tract of land in Indian Territory. The Florida Indian situation seemed settled.

As it turned out, the chiefs who signed the Treaty of Fort Gibson had no authority to do so, and the bulk of the Seminoles refused to honor it. Hostilities grew worse over the next two years. During this time, a young and dynamic part-white/part-Creek warrior whose white name was Powell and whose Seminole name was Osceola emerged as the symbol of Seminole resistance to the relocation plan. In November 1835, events reached the boiling point. An Osceola-led band of Seminoles confronted and murdered Charlie Emathla, one of the chiefs who had signed the Treaty of Fort Gibson and who was preparing to migrate. For the next several weeks, marauding bands of Seminoles attacked and burned some of Florida's largest plantations. White settlers fled to St. Augustine in fear for their lives.

On December 28, 1835, the same day as Dade's Massacre but fifty miles north, near Fort King, Osceola and about thirty warriors stalked Indian agent Wiley Thompson. Thompson had formerly been Osceola's friend, but months earlier, Thompson had slapped Osceola into chains after the two argued. Osceola thus had a personal vendetta against Thompson. Brandishing rifles and tomahawks, Osceola's army shot down and scalped the surprised Thompson and several other whites outside the post. Although previous skirmishes had occurred between the Seminoles and the army, the nearly simultaneous ambushes of Dade and Thompson signaled the onset of an all-out war. The two Seminole forces rendezvoused the next day at the Cove of the Withlacoochee, near the scene of the Dade Massacre. Chiefs Micanopy, Alligator and Jumper, with Osceola, were intent on reclaiming by force the whole of Florida for the Seminole Nation.

From 1836 through 1838, the Seminoles outlasted the American army. A succession of army commanders—Duncan Clinch, Winfield Scott, Richard Keith Call, Thomas S. Jesup and Zachary Taylor—had tried and failed to subdue the amalgamated Florida tribes. The Indians were better at guerrilla warfare and easily melted into swamps and hammocks, where they could outmaneuver the less agile army. As many as 8,400 soldiers and volunteers were in Florida in late 1837, only half of whom were healthy and on duty. But by the time the Seventh Infantry arrived in 1839, fewer than 3,000 remained. Two events stand out from this period: the capture of Osceola under a flag of truce by General Jesup in October 1837 and the three-day Battle of Okeechobee from December 19 through December 21, 1837, which, at least nominally, was won by Colonel Zachary Taylor's 1,000-man force. Taylor, still under Jesup's command at the time, accepted promotion to brevet brigadier general for his success at Okeechobee. Despite Osceola's capture and ultimate death in captivity and Colonel Taylor's Okeechobee victory, the war dragged on. The hit, run and hide tactics of the Seminoles, and the semitropical heat and diseases of Florida, continued to take their toll on the army.[62] Several hundred Seminoles had actually capitulated and immigrated to the West, including Micanopy and Alligator, the two chiefs responsible for Dade's defeat and for the death of John Slade Gatlin, but the Indians who remained in Florida were determined to stay. They continued to pose a constant deadly threat to both the American army and the few thousand white settlers brave enough or foolish enough to remain in Florida.

Captain Benjamin L.E. Bonneville's Company F preceded the rest of the Seventh Infantry to Florida in January 1839.[63] Bonneville had left the regiment some years earlier to explore the Rocky Mountains. Failing to return when expected, he was listed as dead for a time. He returned in 1835 and was reinstated at full rank, much to the consternation of some of the younger officers, Gatlin included, who had hoped to progress in his

Chief Micanopy of the Seminoles. His attack on Dade's command killed John S. Gatlin and 105 other U.S. soldiers. From McKenney and Hall's *History of the Indian Tribes of North America* (1858), based on an 1825 painting by Charles Bird King. *Wikimedia Commons.*

absence.[64] Bonneville would significantly figure into Gatlin's future promotional prospects. The remainder of the regiment soon followed Bonneville to Florida.

Regimental commander Colonel William Whistler, Adjutant Gatlin and nine companies of the Seventh Infantry departed Fort Gibson on February 7, 1839. They marched from Fort Gibson to Fort Smith and then rode keelboats to Little Rock, where the steamer *Arkansas* took them to the Mississippi River and down to New Orleans, their embarkation point for Florida. Low water in the Arkansas River severely delayed their arrival at New Orleans, but finally, after an uneventful voyage across the Gulf of Mexico and more than six weeks after departing Fort Gibson, the Seventh arrived at Fort Brooke at Tampa Bay in two groups on March 24 and March 27, 1839. From Fort Brooke, the companies of the Seventh Infantry were dispatched to various forts and camps in north-central Florida. Whistler, Gatlin, Captain Dixon S. Miles and the men of Company E left Fort Brooke on April 3 to set up regimental headquarters at Fort King near present-day Ocala. In marching from Tampa to Fort King, Gatlin and his battalion followed the same trail taken by Major Dade's unfortunate command just three years earlier. Gatlin undoubtedly recalled his brother's violent death as he crossed the scene of the massacre, but he makes no mention of it in his writings.[65]

With American public opinion souring on the Seminole War, the War Department took the extraordinary approach of sending the commanding general of the U.S. Army, General Alexander Macomb, to Florida with the express hope of arranging a peace. Macomb arrived at the army's supply depot at Garry's Ferry in April, survived a trek across the dangerous military trail from Palatka to Fort Micanopy and arrived at Fort King in mid-May 1839. General Zachary Taylor, who had succeeded Jesup as commander of the Florida army in May 1838, arrived at Fort King about the same time. The Seventh Infantry band at Fort King greeted Macomb and Taylor with all the pomp and circumstance befitting the army's top general, and the officers and men at the fort dressed out in their finest formal uniforms. During his stay, Macomb entertained several of the officers, including Lieutenant Gatlin, with dinner. On May 18, 1839, after meeting with but one Seminole chief, Chitto Tustenuggee, Macomb declared the war at an end and directed that the remaining Seminoles occupy a reservation in the southwestern part of Florida. With his business completed, General Macomb left Florida confident of his success. Of course, it was not long before the declared peace was broken and the hostilities resumed in earnest.

The Seventh Infantry headquarters remained at Fort King until December 4, 1839, when Colonel Whistler moved it to Fort Micanopy near present-day Gainesville in Alachua County.[66] Adjutant Gatlin, headquarters staff and three companies occupied Fort Micanopy. Two companies remained at Fort Brooke, and the remaining five were dispersed to forts in and around Alachua County. "Bloody" Alachua was undoubtedly the most treacherous part of Florida. It was the scene of more skirmishes and casualties than any other place in Florida.[67]

For three years, the Seventh Infantry was involved in some of the bloodiest clashes between the army and the Seminoles. On March 28, 1840, Captain Gabriel J. Rains, commanding Company A, marched from Fort King with fourteen men on a scouting mission. A band of ninety-three warriors

Gabriel Rains of New Bern, North Carolina, longtime U.S. Seventh Infantry officer and Confederate general. *Library of Congress.*

ambushed his party, killing two men in the initial volley. Rains re-formed his remaining men and broke free, but in the escape attempt, he fell severely wounded. Three of his men dragged him back to the fort. The Florida newspapers called this the most gallant action of the war, and Captain Rains was brevetted to major for his conduct. Gatlin might have been with Rains during this engagement. One account states, "Captain Rains had been too badly wounded on the 28th of April to make a report of his fight with the enemy. Lieutenant R.C. Gatlin, adjutant of the Seventh Infantry, on returning to camp, furnished Colonel Whistler with the details incorporated in the report."[68]

On May 19, 1840, eight miles from Fort King, a band of approximately one hundred warriors attacked a detachment led by Lieutenant James S. Sanderson of Company C and killed five men, including Lieutenant Sanderson.[69]

In June 1840, Captain Bonneville led a probe into Big Swamp, fifteen miles from Fort King, where he surprised and scattered a band of one hundred Indians engaged in the Green Corn Dance.[70]

The most disturbing encounter occurred on December 28, 1840, five years to the day after Dade's Massacre. A patrol consisting of Second Lieutenant Walter Sherwood of Company K, Second Lieutenant Nevil Hopson of Company G, Sergeant Major Francis Carroll and ten privates left Fort Micanopy escorting Mrs. Elizabeth Montgomery, young bride of Lieutenant Alexander Montgomery of Company C, to Fort Waccahoota, only eight miles away, for a social visit. About halfway into the journey, Seminoles surprised the detachment and killed two privates instantly. Mrs. Montgomery dismounted her horse, hoping to hide in the wagon, but an attacker's bullet found and killed her. Lieutenant Hopson galloped back to Micanopy for reinforcements while Lieutenant Sherwood and the rest of the survivors fought hand to hand with the Indians. The war party overwhelmed, killed and scalped Sherwood, Sergeant Major Carroll and four privates and then mutilated Mrs. Montgomery's body. One private, still alive but dying when Lieutenant Montgomery and a relief unit arrived, assured the horrified Lieutenant Montgomery that he had done his best to protect Mrs. Montgomery. His last words were, "I did my duty."[71]

By the spring of 1842, few enough Seminoles remained in Florida that the new commander, General William J. Worth, whom Gatlin had accompanied on board the *Telegraph* during the Patriot's War three and a half years earlier, declared victory and an end to the hostilities. The army began leaving Florida, and Gatlin himself left in March 1842 for a four-month furlough in North Carolina.[72] During its three years in Florida, the Seventh Infantry lost 2 officers killed in battle and 2 from disease; 28 of the rank and file were killed by Indians, and 116 died from disease.[73]

While on leave in North Carolina, Gatlin revisited old acquaintances in Kinston and spent time with his mother and sister in Everettsville before rejoining his regiment in garrison at New Orleans Barracks, Louisiana, in July 1842.[74] The visit with his mother was Gatlin's last, for she would die nine months later at the home of Ann and Reverend Hooks in Everettsville on

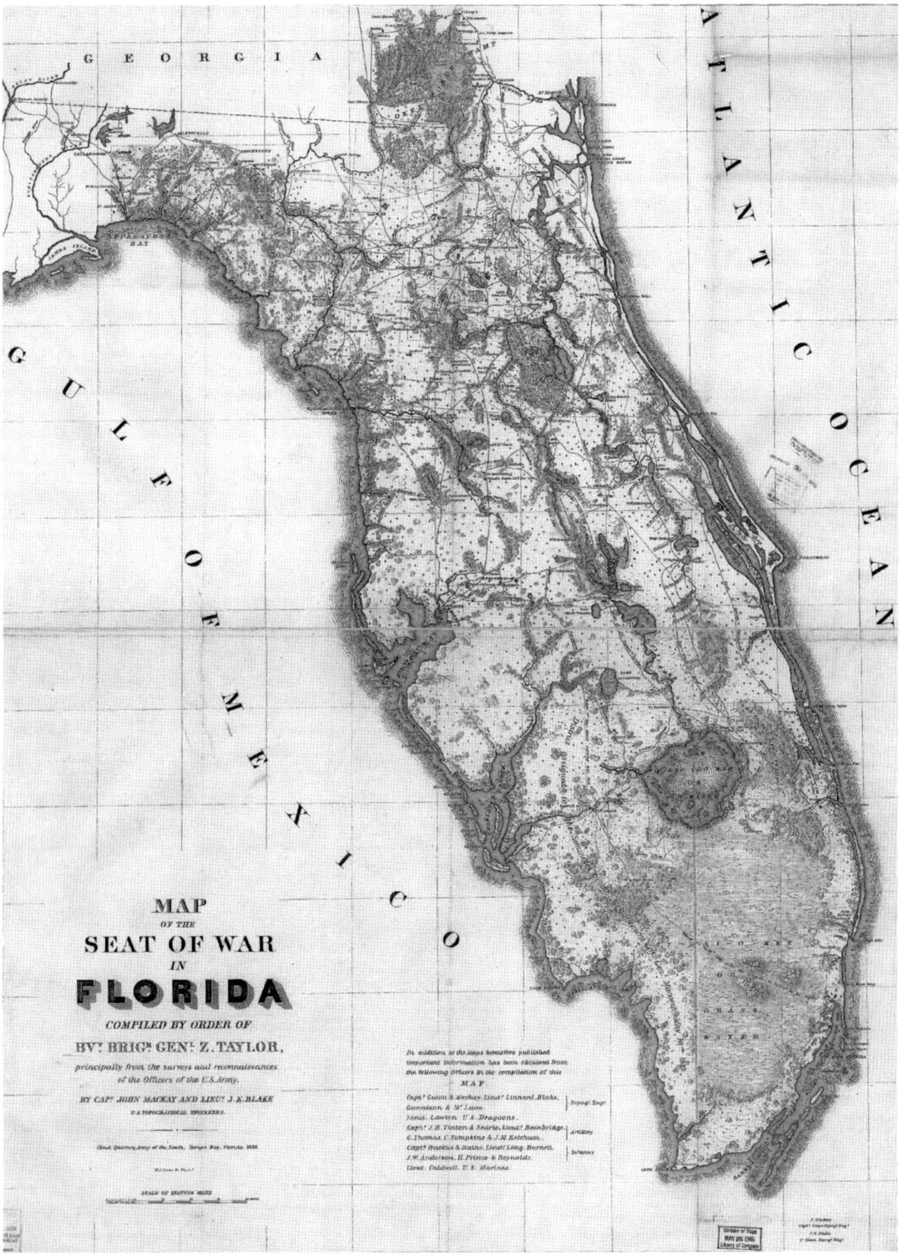

A map of Florida during the Second Seminole War compiled in 1839 by order of Brevet Brigadier General Zachary Taylor. *State Archives of Florida.*

March 5, 1843. Susannah Gatlin was buried near Kinston beside her famous father at the Caswell Cemetery on the Red House Plantation.[75] Richard Gatlin was thirty-four years old and still unmarried, and of his entire family, only he and two of his sisters, Mary Knox in St. Louis and Ann Hooks in Everettsville, remained.

The summer after reporting to his new duty station, the heat and humidity of the Louisiana climate triggered a recurrence of the malaria Gatlin had suffered several years before in Indian Territory. Too unwell to perform his duties to his satisfaction, Gatlin left New Orleans on June 10, 1843, for an extended sick leave to White Sulphur Springs in the mountains of Virginia. A summer and fall in the high country of Virginia seemed to restore his vitality, and Gatlin returned to his regiment on November 13, 1843. For the next twenty-one months, he was constantly at the side of General Arbuckle, performing adjutant duties as the regiment alternated between New Orleans Barracks in the cooler months and Camp Pass Christian, Mississippi, during the heat of summer.[76]

Chapter 7

"Halls of the Montezumas": The Mexican War

In 1844, John O'Sullivan had not yet coined the term "Manifest Destiny," but the concept it embraced, that of extending the virtues of liberty across the entire North American continent as one United States from the Atlantic to the Pacific, was certainly clear in many people's minds. The United States at the time was bursting with pride and ambition, but an ominous cloud lurked over it as well. The early 1840s was a chaotic era in which political issues promised to expand and social issues threatened to split the United States. Dark horse Democrat James K. Polk won the 1844 presidential election with his famous "54-40 or Fight" campaign. The previous year, significant numbers of pioneers had begun trekking the trans–Rocky Mountain trail to the Oregon Territory, over which the United States and Britain were involved in a territorial dispute. The Compromise of 1820 had only temporarily calmed the political upheaval of slavery, and a surging abolitionist movement from the North was beginning to disturb southerners. The country was polarized on the slavery issue. Talk of annexing Texas and adding Florida as a state alarmed those opposed to extending slavery. It also alarmed the Mexican government, which viewed American annexation of Texas as a direct incursion on its territory. Polk compromised with the British on the Oregon issue, but relations with Mexico deteriorated.

In July 1845, after the annexation of Texas but before it became a state, Polk, on the alert for Mexican reprisal, ordered General Zachary Taylor and much of the U.S. Army, 3,500 men, to Corpus Christi as the Army of Observation.[77] The August 22, 1845 issue of the *New Orleans*

View from Fort Texas looking out at Matamoros across the Rio Grande, 1846. *University of Texas–Arlington.*

Picayune announced the departure from New Orleans of Seventh Infantry Companies B, C, F, H and I, plus Lieutenant Gatlin and Surgeon Craig, on board the steamship *Alabama* bound for Texas.[78] Most of the Seventh Infantry, including Gatlin, arrived at Corpus Christi on August 30, 1845.[79] Gatlin was still adjutant and a first lieutenant, but Bonneville had been promoted to major and transferred to the Fourth Infantry,[80] thus creating an opening in the Seventh Infantry for a captain and a new commander for Bonneville's Company F. Next in line for the post was Gatlin's old West Point classmate Roger Dix. Dix, however, had been on detached service with the Quartermaster Corps in Louisiana since 1838, had already been a captain since July 1845 and was not inclined to return to field command, where promotions came more slowly. He refused the assignment and transferred permanently to the Quartermaster Corps.[81] Consequently, the opportunity fell to Gatlin. In October 1845, Gatlin accepted a promotion to captain, effective September 30, 1845; relinquished his role as adjutant; and took command of Company F.[82] It had taken him thirteen years to reach command grade, just about the average in the antebellum army. Captain Gatlin's subalterns in Company F were First Lieutenant Forbes Britton, an 1834 West Point graduate from Virginia who had distinguished himself in the Seminole War, and Second Lieutenant Levi Gantt, an 1841 West Point graduate from the District of Columbia.

Corpus Christi became a city of tents, as is evident in a contemporary painting by Gatlin's old friend and classmate Captain Daniel Powers Whiting. Whiting was commanding the Seventh Infantry's Company K when he sketched a now-famous scene of row upon row of neatly aligned white tents lined up on the Corpus Christi beach.[83] For six long months,

A bird's-eye view (looking north) of the camp of the Army of Occupation, commanded by General Taylor, near Corpus Christi, Texas, October 1845. Painted by Gatlin's friend and fellow officer D.P. Whiting. *Library of Congress.*

the men of the Seventh Infantry lived in this camp, infested with snakes and scorpions. Finally, when it appeared that the Mexicans were amassing their army under General Pedro de Ampudia across the Rio Grande at the city of Matamoros, the men struck their tents in March 1846 and, in three brigades led by General Taylor, General William Worth and Colonel Whistler, dispatched the army southward.

The Army of Observation established camp at present-day Brownsville, across the Rio Grande from the Mexican city of Matamoros, and assumed the name of "Army of Occupation." The men of the Seventh Infantry began constructing an earthen fort that General Taylor named Fort Texas.[84] During this time, some troops and slaves took advantage of their proximity to Mexico and tried to escape to the Mexican side. Some were successful, and some lost their lives in the attempt. Lieutenant Napoleon Dana wrote to his wife, "I did not tell you of some of the Negro servants running away from camp. Gatlin lost his boy and Major Rains' Sandy has gone too, and several others."[85] On April 25, 1846, the Mexicans crossed to the north side of the Rio Grande and ambushed an American dragoon detachment, killing eleven Americans and capturing several more.[86] Word of the attack reached Washington two weeks later. As a result, Congress declared war on Mexico on May 13, 1846.[87] By that date, however, General Taylor had already taken the war to the Mexicans.

On May 1, Taylor left the Seventh Infantry and two companies of artillery to finish constructing and garrison Fort Texas and marched the bulk of his army eastward to Point Isabel, where his supply base was unprotected. With Taylor gone, the Mexican artillery in Matamoros opened fire on Fort Texas and on the men of the Seventh Infantry inside. From Point Isabel, Taylor's army could hear the artillery fire resounding from both sides of the Rio Grande. Second Lieutenant Ulysses S. Grant, with Taylor's force in the Fourth Infantry, was shaken on hearing the muffled thunder of war for the first time. He later wrote in his memoirs, "What General Taylor's feelings were during this suspense I do not know; but for myself, a young second-lieutenant who had never heard a hostile gun before, I felt sorry that I had enlisted."[88]

The Mexicans laid siege to the fort for seven days from May 3 to May 9, but the American artillery, manned by Lieutenants Braxton Bragg, George H. Thomas and John F. Reynolds, effectively held them at bay. Captain Gatlin and the other officers hastily directed the construction of bomb proofs and redoubts inside the fort, which kept the casualty toll low. Major Jacob Brown, commanding the Seventh, and one sergeant were the only Americans killed in the siege. An incoming cannonball smashed Major

Brown's leg, and an amputation was unsuccessful in saving his life.[89] At some point, young and impetuous Seventh Infantry lieutenant Earl Van Dorn gained lasting notoriety among the defenders when he rushed out of the fort, dodged cannonballs and whistling bullets and ran a fallen American flag up a flagpole situated outside.

Meanwhile, General Taylor, satisfied that Point Isabel was secure, turned his army around and marched back toward Fort Texas. He encountered the Mexican army on May 7, 1846, before reaching the fort and routed them at the Battles of Palo Alto and Resaca de Palma, sending them back across the Rio Grande in disarray.[90] Thus, the siege of Fort Texas ended, and the Mexican War was on in full fury. At least twelve future Civil War generals were among the defenders inside Fort Texas during the siege, including Gatlin, Braxton Bragg, T.H. Holmes, Earl Van Dorn, LaFayette McLaws, Franklin Gardner and Gabriel Rains, who would later wear gray, and Joseph K.F. Mansfield, George H. Thomas, Joseph Potter, John F. Reynolds and Napoleon Dana, who would lead the North.[91] Also at the fort, hauling ammunition and tending the wounded, was six-foot-tall camp laundress Sarah Bourginnis, whose size, bravery and later legendary exploits earned her a commission in the U.S. Army and the sobriquet "Great Western." Fort Texas was renamed Fort Brown for its fallen commander, and the town of Brownsville, Texas, later grew up around it.

Rather than pursuing the fleeing Mexicans, Taylor occupied Matamoros for several days and then led his growing army up the Rio Grande. He established a supply base at the town of Camargo on a tributary of the Rio Grande in June and waited through July and August for men and supplies to reach him. In September, he began a southwesterly move toward Monterrey, where General Ampudia had gathered his army. Gatlin, confident of a quick American victory, remarked to Lieutenant Napoleon Dana that he would "take his Christmas dinner in the halls of the Montezumas."[92]

With six thousand men in three divisions, Taylor attacked the strongly defended Monterrey on Monday, September 21, 1846. Boldly splitting his force, he sent General William J. Worth's division to attack Monterrey from the west, while he and the remaining two divisions attacked from the east. Worth had been Gatlin's commander twice before, aboard the *Telegraph* back in 1838 during the Patriot's War and again during the Seminole War. He was Gatlin's commander again as the Seventh Infantry made up part of his division.[93] During the next two days and nights, often in a cold, driving rain, Worth's division pressed into Monterrey while Taylor was being repulsed on the east side of the city. By Wednesday, September 23, 1846, Taylor's

Gatlin's Mexican War commander, Major General Zachary Taylor. *Library of Congress.*

superior artillery had gained him the upper hand in the east, while Gatlin and the Seventh Infantry were fighting street to street and house to house, taking heavy fire from the retreating *soldados* in the west.[94] While leading Company F through a hail of bullets in an assault through the streets of Monterrey, Gatlin took a musket ball through the left shoulder, knocking him out of action.[95] Caught between the two American divisions, Taylor on the east and Worth on the west, General Ampudia surrendered the city to Taylor on September 24, 1846. General Taylor, to the dismay of President Polk, liberally allowed the Mexican army to retain its hand weapons and march away from Monterrey. Gatlin's wound was serious but not life threatening. He earned a battlefield promotion to brevet major and a commendation for meritorious conduct[96] and tried to recuperate in Monterrey. In October 1846, Gatlin chose to return home once again to recuperate rather than remain in the field hospital.[97] He arrived by steamboat in New Orleans in November 1846 and remained only briefly before setting out for Kinston.

American soldiers storming Palace Hill at the Battle of Monterrey, September 22, 1846. Gatlin was wounded the following day. *Lithograph by Kelloggs & Thayer; Library of Congress.*

Still recovering from his shoulder wound, Gatlin sailed from New Orleans to North Carolina, arriving home on January 24, 1847. The trip was reminiscent of the one he had made fourteen years earlier as an injured young brevet second lieutenant from Fort Gibson. After a brief visit with his sister Ann Hooks in Everettsville, he rode up to Raleigh to meet with Governor William A. Graham. Graham was from Lincolnton, North Carolina, and made his home in Hillsborough in Orange County, North Carolina, but he had a Kinston connection. His wife was Susan Washington, the daughter of John Washington, one of Kinston's most esteemed citizens of the previous generation and a distant relative of President George Washington. The Gatlin and Washington families had been close friends in Kinston, and Richard Gatlin was distantly related to the governor's wife. Governor Graham had asked Gatlin to come to Raleigh to offer him a colonelcy and command of the newly forming First North Carolina Volunteers. Gatlin courteously declined, saying of that offer, "Gov. Graham offered me the Colcy of the No. Carolina Volunteers, but Secty of War (Marcy) expressing permission to hold on to my commission in the Army was forced to decline."[98] At that point, at least, Gatlin preferred federal service to home state service. The next time that option arose, he would choose differently.

In February 1847, as soon as he fully recovered, Gatlin made the arduous journey back to Mexico to rejoin his unit and resume command of his company. He got as far as Vera Cruz, where he learned that he had been reassigned to recruiting duty in the States.[99] Returning to New Orleans, he lingered long enough to have a daguerreotype made of himself in his captain's uniform and to arrange to go on recruiting trips to Louisville and Boston.

From February through November 1847, Gatlin busily mustered in new recruits in New Orleans, Louisville and Boston. His first stop was the recruiting depot at Louisville, Kentucky. The Fourth Indiana Volunteers were being raised in Jeffersonville, Indiana, across the Ohio River from Louisville. Gatlin personally mustered in a large number of these recruits during late May, June and July. From Kentucky, Gatlin traveled on to Boston, where, in the crisp New England fall, he undoubtedly sold many young Irish immigrants on the wonders of Mexico and the virtues of serving in the United States Army. While at Boston, he called on his friend First Lieutenant Napoleon Dana, who was now a brevet captain. Dana had been severely wounded in the Battle of Cerro Gordo in April 1847 and, as a result, was reassigned to recruiting duty until he could regain his health. By the end of October, Gatlin received orders to gather his contingent of eager new warriors in New York and sail for Mexico. Departing New York in November 1847, Gatlin's little army arrived in Vera Cruz on the Mexican coast in the latter part of December. They proudly marched into Mexico City on January 20, 1848.[100] Gatlin describes his entire recruiting service of that period with only these words: "Served on that duty in N.O., Louisville and Boston until 31st Octr when I was ordered to conduct recruits from N.Y. to Mexico. While at Louisville mustered into the service the 4th Indiana Regiment in July and a mounted company at Shawnee Town in August."[101]

By the time Gatlin and his recruits reached Mexico City on January 20, 1848, the fighting had ceased. The Treaty of Guadalupe Hidalgo officially ended the war less than two weeks later. Reassuming command of Company F, Gatlin learned that his subaltern, First Lieutenant Forbes Britton, was now a captain and was serving as brigade quartermaster. He also learned that Second Lieutenant Levi Gantt, while commanding Company F in Gatlin's absence, had died in action on September 13, 1847, at the Battle of Chapultepec. Most of Gatlin's other Seventh Infantry cohorts had survived the war. Captain Dixon S. Miles had commanded the regiment during the siege of Vera Cruz in May 1847 and served as commander of the city of Vera Cruz from August 1847 to December 1847. Captain T.H. Holmes, after participating in the Siege of Vera Cruz, had gone on recruiting duty in the States. Captain Charles H. Humber had survived a severe wound at the Battle of Contreras in August 1847 and went to Jefferson Barracks, Missouri. Majors Edgar Hawkins and Gabriel Rains had both left Mexico on recruiting duty after the Siege of Fort Texas. Hawkins had subsequently gone on an extended sickness furlough. In other sad news, Gatlin learned that the army had cashiered Lieutenant Nevil Hopson from service before the

Captain Richard C. Gatlin on furlough in New Orleans, 1847. *North Carolina Museum of History.*

Battle of Monterrey, but he had stayed in Texas and had died in 1847 at age thirty-two.

Future controversial Confederate general Earl Van Dorn had made quite a name for himself with a promotion to first lieutenant in March 1847, a brevet to captain for his actions in the Battle of Cerro Gordo in April 1847 and another brevet to major for his actions in the Battles of Contreras and Churubusco in August 1847.

Major Roger Dix, who had chosen to remain with the quartermaster corps, did not escape combat. His gallant and meritorious service in the Battle of Buena Vista in February 1847 earned him a brevet to lieutenant colonel.

Finally, Captain Daniel P. Whiting had been engaged in the Siege of Vera Cruz in March 1847 and the Battle of Cerro Gordo in April 1847, for which he was brevetted major for gallant and meritorious service. After the Battle of Cerro Gordo, he received orders for recruiting duty and escaped the war unscathed. While Whiting was on recruiting service at Louisville, Kentucky, his wife, Indiana, gave birth to a son, their sixth child. Whiting recorded in his diary, "On the 3d of May, 1848, another son was vouchsafed to us and we called him Richard Gatlin after our esteemed friend, my fellow classmate and brother officer in the Regiment."[102]

Because of his notable Mexican War service, Gatlin's fellow officers elected him as a charter member of the Aztec Club, an elite social organization of Mexican War officers that met for years after the Mexican and Civil Wars. Among the most recognizable names of other charter members are Robert E. Lee, U.S. Grant, Franklin Pierce, Zachary Taylor, Winfield Scott and George B. McClellan. Grandsons continue the Aztec Club as a military descendants club to this day.[103]

Chapter 8

"Gloomy Endurance of a Shrouded Future": Mid-Century Joy and Tragedy

On June 6, 1848, the Seventh Infantry began leaving Mexico with Gatlin in command of Companies F, G and H.[104] The regiment alternately marched and camped through Mexico until they reached the Mexican coast at Vera Cruz, where Gatlin's three companies boarded the transport *Creole* on July 7, 1848. They arrived at New Orleans on July 9, 1848; took a steamer the same day up the Mississippi River; and arrived at Jefferson Barracks near St. Louis, Missouri, on July 27, 1848.[105] As the senior officer on duty, Gatlin served as regimental commander from August 1 until August 12, when his old friend Brevet Major T.H. Holmes relieved him.[106]

On October 6, 1848, Brevet Major Gatlin was on the river again, with his Company F, bound for Baton Rouge Barracks, Louisiana, and special duty with Zachary Taylor.[107] Taylor, who had quickly parlayed his Mexican War fame into the Whig candidacy for president, was campaigning for the upcoming 1848 election from his home in Baton Rouge. Gatlin, with Earl Van Dorn and Company F, remained in Baton Rouge until May 1849,[108] leaving only after Taylor had won the November election and had departed for his inauguration in March 1849.

Upon arriving at Jefferson Barracks in May 1849, Gatlin's life took an amorous turn. His longtime friend and fellow Seventh Infantry officer Daniel Powers Whiting had been on recruiting duty in Covington, Kentucky, in 1834 when he met and married eighteen-year-old Indiana Sandford, daughter of Alfred Sandford.[109] In 1835, Alfred Sandford moved west to St. Louis with his remaining four daughters and three sons.[110] In 1844, Alfred Sandford's second daughter, twenty-three-year-old Susan Lewis Martin Sandford, had married Seventh Infantry lieutenant Napoleon Jackson Tecumseh Dana in New Orleans.[111] On May 25, 1849, just days after Gatlin's return from Baton Rouge Barracks, Indiana Whiting died in childbirth at Jefferson Barracks. Her husband, D.P. Whiting, wrote, "On the 25th of May, 1849, my wife died. After a two day's illness, in child-birth, my Indie left me forever to a lone and gloomy endurance of a shrouded future."[112] Gatlin had been courting twenty-two-year-old Scioto Sandford, one of Indiana Whiting's younger sisters, and he now consoled both his widowed friend Whiting and a bereaved Scioto.

Later that summer, on August 16, 1849, forty-year-old Brevet Major Richard Caswell Gatlin and Scioto Sandford, the fourth of Alfred Sandford's five daughters, were married at Jefferson Barracks.[113] It is difficult to say how long Gatlin had wooed Scioto, for he left no written record of the courtship or the marriage. As Whiting's close friend, however, Gatlin had known all the Sandfords for years and had seen Scioto blossom from a child into young womanhood. Scioto was the third of Alfred Sandford's daughters to marry a Seventh Infantry officer, and Gatlin, Whiting and Dana, comrades-in-arms, became brothers-in-law. Whiting, with older children to care for, left his one-year-old son, Richard Gatlin Whiting, in Gatlin and Scioto's care.[114]

From August to November 1849, Gatlin honeymooned with his new bride and then hastened to rejoin his regiment, now in Florida. A minor incident involving some independently acting Seminole Indians—they had burned a store and killed the storekeeper and a couple other white men—alarmed the federal government. The army dispatched the Seventh Infantry to Florida to build a string of forts and to quell the insurrection.[115]

Leaving Scioto in St. Louis, Gatlin again crossed the Gulf of Mexico and rejoined his company at the Little Alafia River near Tampa on November 20, 1849. He and his men patrolled the road to the Peace River until January 2, 1850, when they boarded the transport *Colonel Clay* and steamed down the gulf to Charlotte Harbor on the southwest Florida coast. On January 3, 1850, Gatlin took temporary command of newly built Fort Casey on Useppa Island.[116] Fort Casey was isolated and lonely, the duty dull, and the Indians posed no danger. As he so often did throughout their careers, Major T.H. Holmes arrived and relieved Gatlin of command in April, but Gatlin and his company remained until the entire garrison abandoned the fort in June 1850.[117] Just as quickly as it had rushed to Florida, the army pulled out.

Gatlin arrived at Jefferson Barracks in late June 1850, in time to witness the birth of his first son, Johnny Gatlin, on July 12, 1850.[118]

As rapidly as things were changing for Gatlin, they were changing for the United States as well. The Wilmot Proviso in 1846 had threatened but failed to prohibit slavery in any territory gained from the Mexican War. An alarmed southern contingent led by South Carolina senator John C. Calhoun countered in 1847 with a set of resolutions that would have ensured slavery in the territories.[119] The tenuous peace of the Missouri Compromise was ending. The country was splitting over the slavery issue. In the meantime, the Mormons had fled from Illinois to the Rocky Mountains, where they were developing the theocratic nation of Deseret. The gold discovery in California in 1848 precipitated a mad rush of people to the West. Railroads began to crisscross the more populated eastern states, and the newly invented telegraph was promising to introduce instantaneous communication.

On July 9, 1850, President Taylor, who, despite being a southerner and a slave owner himself, had opposed the legalization of slavery in the territories, died in office. His death cleared the way for the Compromise of 1850, which allowed the admission of California to the Union as a free state and created the Utah and New Mexico Territories with no antislavery regulations. Still the southern states fumed with talk of withdrawing from the Union.

Just a month after Johnny Gatlin was born, his father left for Fort Leavenworth to join an expedition to New Mexico. Gatlin left Jefferson Barracks on August 17, 1850; arrived at Fort Leavenworth; and marched with the expedition past the Little Arkansas River en route to Santa Fe. However, the army unexpectedly halted the expedition in October and ordered the men back to Leavenworth. On October 29, 1850, Gatlin returned to Jefferson Barracks, where he remained with his young wife and new son for the next six months.[120] In the spring of 1851, the army redeployed the Seventh Infantry from Jefferson Barracks to various posts across the Southwest.[121]

On April 17, 1851, Gatlin, his wife and son and Companies B and F left Jefferson Barracks on the steamer *Grand Fork* bound for New Orleans. At New Orleans, the party boarded the steamer *Cleona* on April 24, 1851, for the trip back up the Mississippi to the Arkansas River and up the Arkansas to Fort Smith. After various delays, they arrived at Fort Smith on May 14, 1851.[122] Gatlin became regimental recruiting officer upon arrival and assumed command of Fort Smith from Captain C.C. Sibley of the Fifth Infantry on June 6.[123] At Fort Smith, Gatlin reunited with the old warhorse General

Matthew Arbuckle, but only briefly, for Arbuckle died on June 11, 1851, less than a month after Gatlin's arrival.[124] A passing of the torch occurred around 1850 as several of Gatlin's former commanders died about that time. In addition to Arbuckle, General William J. Worth had died of cholera in San Antonio in 1849, President Zachary Taylor had died in office in 1850 and Colonel Richard B. Mason had died in 1850 at Jefferson Barracks after having been military governor of California in 1848–49. In addition, Gatlin's classmate Major Roger Dix, who had passed up the captaincy and command that had gone to Gatlin in 1845, died of cholera near Uniontown, Pennsylvania, in 1849 on his way to Washington, D.C., from Mexico.[125]

For Brevet Major Richard C. Gatlin, however, life could not have been more promising than it was in the summer and fall of 1851. His career was advancing, he had achieved command of a significant post, he was a dedicated husband and father and he had a second child on the way. After almost twenty years in the army, the forty-two-year-old Gatlin had forged a good life in the service. Scioto Gatlin bore a second son on December 27, 1851, at Fort Smith, but the birth was a difficult one, and Scioto died a week later on January 3, 1852. Devoid of his mother, the infant, whom the parents had named Alfred Sandford Gatlin after Scioto's father, followed Scioto into death on January 11, 1852, at fifteen days of age.[126] Gatlin interred Scioto and her son together in a single grave at Fort Smith. Grief-stricken but ever mindful of duty, Gatlin continued his command at Fort Smith only long enough to arrange for a change of venue. D.P. Whiting traveled from Fort Towson to visit Gatlin at Fort Smith in April 1852 and, with Scioto gone, retrieved his son, five-year-old Richard Gatlin Whiting. Of this period, Gatlin says little. In his extant papers, he recorded only: "Remained in command of that post until May 20th, '52 when I was relieved by Col. Wilson. Left Fort Smith July 12th, '52 for General Recruiting Service and entered upon that duty at St. Louis Sept 1st, '52."[127]

Gatlin remained in St. Louis on recruiting duty for the next seventeen months with his remaining son Johnny as a constant companion. On February 16, 1854, Gatlin and three-year-old Johnny boarded the steamer *Kate Kearney* at St. Louis for a short trip up the Mississippi River to Alton, Illinois. An acquaintance, Major Don Carlos Buell of the Quartermaster Corps, also happened to be on board that day. As the *Kate Kearney* slowly eased away from the dock, one of her boilers creaked, hissed and then exploded with a tremendous thunder, spewing steam and iron missiles into the air. Scores of people were instantly pierced, scalded, killed or blown overboard by the blast.[128] Buell and Gatlin were both injured, Buell more seriously than

Gatlin's son Johnny was killed when a steamboat such as these exploded in 1854. *Courtesy of www.steamboattimes.com.*

Gatlin, but both fought the ensuing fire and helped restore some semblance of order.[129] Unfortunate young Johnny Gatlin had been in the wrong place, however. As soon as he realized that Johnny was hurt, Gatlin picked up his seriously burned son and rushed him ashore to the nearest St. Louis hospital. Johnny lingered for ten days, but on February 26, 1854, Richard Gatlin's only surviving son died from his scalding injuries.[130] Gatlin remained in St. Louis until August 1, 1854, and then took a four-month furlough, traveling back east. His exact itinerary during the next few months is unclear, but he wrote, "Relieved at St. Louis by Capt. Dent 1st Aug. 1854. Obtained a furlough for four months. Went on Court Martial at Charleston in Nov. 54. To try Dr. Porter."[131]

In February 1855, Gatlin ended his extended stay in the Carolinas and headed north to one of the army's main recruiting centers, Newport Barracks, Kentucky, with orders to take charge of a detachment of 283 recruits destined for Fort Gibson and service in the Seventh Infantry. Lieutenant Colonel Pitcairn Morrison urgently needed the recruits for a summer expedition to the Big Timbers of Colorado that he was planning.[132] Gatlin, ever the soldier, was ready to return to command. The weather worked against him, however, for when he and his recruits reached Pine

Bluff, Arkansas, on the Arkansas River in April 1855, the river was too low to accommodate any traffic. With all their supplies and equipment on board a steamboat, the detachment was stuck near Pine Bluff for nearly two months. According to Gatlin, his troops subsisted on salt pork this entire time, and a majority came down with scurvy while waiting for the river to rise.[133] The big stream did eventually rise, and Gatlin's detachment was able to proceed. They reached Fort Gibson on June 10, 1855.[134]

In 1837, Captain Pitcairn Morrison had escorted the captive Seminole warrior Osceola from Florida to Fort Moultrie, South Carolina, where Osceola starved himself to death. Now, on June 22, 1855, Morrison led three companies of Seventh Infantry, including Gatlin's Company F, across the Santa Fe Trail to Bent's Fort in the Big Timbers country of present-day Colorado. The expedition was designed to intimidate the Plains Indians into ceasing their depredations against the growing number of travelers destined for New Mexico. Having spent the summer meeting with Kiowa, Comanche, Arapaho, Apache and Cheyenne councils to little avail, Morrison, Gatlin and the two-hundred-plus men of the battalion retraced their steps to Fort Gibson, arriving on October 25, 1855.[135]

Gatlin left Fort Gibson in December 1855 when the army reassigned him and Companies B and F of the Seventh Infantry to Fort Smith. The army had nearly closed Fort Smith due to obsolescence in 1854, but the people of Arkansas protested so vigorously that the federal government consented to let it remain open and garrison it with a skeleton force in late 1855.[136] Arriving on December 8, 1855, Gatlin took command of Fort Smith for the second time—but only temporarily, for in January 1856, Major Isaac Lynde of the Seventh Infantry arrived and assumed command of the post. Gatlin would again command Fort Smith from March 1856 to December 1856 and from June 1857 to August 1857 at times when Major Lynde was absent.[137]

His letters to his sister Mary in California show that Gatlin was moving on from the deaths of his wife and sons. On July 26, 1856, he wrote:

> *I have received your letter of the 24th…also Sarah's sweet picture* [Mary's daughter]…*I have but little news from this secluded country…We have had a wedding, Shingo Rector to Lt. Cabell…a bridal party is to take place…the weather is very scorching…as I am just the weight of a barrel of flour, I shall stay home and let the younger gentlemen go…Mrs. Gibson is living on her farm...She has a very lovely daughter named Mary who is a great favorite of mine.*[138]

The "lovely" object of Gatlin's attention was twenty-year-old Mary Ann Gibson, the daughter of Robert Stuart Gibson, who had died in 1845, and Sarah Price Perkins Nicks Gibson. Sarah Gibson, more commonly known as Sallie, had come to Arkansas as a young girl in the 1820s. In 1824, she married General John Nicks, former Seventh Infantry major and then the sutler at Cantonment Gibson. Much older than Sallie, Nicks died in 1830, and the widow was courted by most of the single men at Fort Gibson. In 1835, she married Nicks's partner, Robert S. Gibson, and daughter Mary Ann was born the following year.[139] Mary Ann was indeed a great favorite of Gatlin's, and he must have been a great favorite of hers as well. On January 20, 1857, Gatlin and Mary Ann Gibson were married at the home of Mary Ann's sister and brother-in-law, Elizabeth Nicks and Samuel S. Griffith, in Fort Smith.[140]

Chapter 9

"A Great Event Has Happened": Into the West and Back

By 1847, the young Church of Jesus Christ of the Latter Day Saints, known as the Mormons, under the leadership of charismatic Governor Brigham Young, had found its way to the Utah Territory and had begun building a new realm. Practically from the time of its founding by Joseph Smith in New York in 1830, the Mormon Church had drawn antipathy from non-Mormons. Distrustful of the Mormons' closed and tightly knit society and resentful of its practice of polygamy and of its extra-Biblical tenets, many "gentiles" viewed Mormonism as dangerously radical. Encountering hostility in every locality in which they settled, the Mormons had felt compelled, as a group, to migrate westward across the country from one state to another. In 1839, they established themselves in Commerce, Illinois; renamed the town Nauvoo; and spent the next five years developing a thriving community. Then, in 1844, a mob from surrounding towns attacked Nauvoo and shot and killed Joseph Smith. Soon afterward, the Mormons abandoned Nauvoo, wandered west and finally found solitude along the Great Salt Lake in 1847. For the next ten years, they industriously went about the business of developing their high mountain homeland into a paradise on earth, and by 1857, they had built Utah into a burgeoning theocracy.[111]

Despite their isolation in Utah and their vast distance from the populated regions of the United States, the Mormons continued to upset large factions back east. Perhaps most disturbing to non-Mormons was the prospect of the Mormons establishing their own independent state, which they intended to do, having gone so far as to designate its name—

Mountain man Jim Bridger, whom Gatlin knew briefly while at Fort Bridger. *Courtesy of www.promfih.com.*

Deseret. Thus, in 1857, the newly elected president, James Buchanan, found himself under extreme political pressure to resolve the perceived Mormon problem. Buchanan decided to exercise governmental control over Mormon Utah by replacing Governor Brigham Young with an appointed governor from outside Utah. His choice for the job was Alfred Cumming of Georgia.

President Buchanan dispatched Cumming, with his family and staff, to Utah in September 1857 in an escort of 2,500 men under the command of Colonel Albert Sidney Johnston. When Young learned of his deposal and that the Johnston expedition was on its way to Utah, he declared martial law in Utah and urged his people to resist—the so-called Utah War had begun. In consequence of these events, the western army went into motion.

Gatlin's Company F transferred to Fort Laramie in the Nebraska Territory on the old Oregon Trail between Fort Leavenworth and Salt Lake.[112] He and the pregnant Mary Ann, along with their servants, left Fort Smith by wagon on August 1, 1857, and arrived at Fort Laramie on September 26, just in time for Mary Ann to give birth to a daughter.[113] Describing the trip in a letter to his sister on October 18, 1857, Gatlin says:

> *Our journey from Fort Smith was a very long and tedious one. Consuming near two months, and amount*[ing] *to an Emigration over land of about 1000 miles. We brought our household goods and servants—Prov and his wife and a little Negro girl, Sally...Since our arrival a great event has happened in the family: nothing less than the birth of a daughter who I have named Susan Caswell, after our dear mother...She was born at Fort Laramie, Nebraska Territory Oct. 11, 1857...This Post is on the Laramie River at the foot of the Black Hills, about 640 miles from Fort Leavenworth and 550 miles from Salt Lake...The Expedition to Salt Lake City is the absorbing subject in these parts...Col. Johnston who is in command left here about twelve days ago.*[114]

Wintering in the Black Hills appears to have agreed with Gatlin, for on January 18, 1858, he wrote to his sister:

> *Mary enjoys most excellent health...Prov and his wife are also in fine health...I am about the heaviest man at the post...I enjoy uninterrupted good health...Indeed I think were I to visit Kinston the old Negroes might with truth say that I look just like "Old Master"...Our Army were not able to reach Salt Lake City this winter owing to the lateness of the season, the loss of animals and the opposition of the Mormons. They are encamped near Fort Bridger some 130 miles from the city.*[115]

Icy-cold blizzards and the Mormons had halted Johnston's approach during the winter, but as spring broke, the army moved to Salt Lake City, and the Mormons fled southward to Provo. Young relented and turned the Utah government over to his appointed successor, Cumming, in April 1858, thus ending the Utah War without bloodshed. For the next two years, the army occupied the Utah Territory in relative peace with the Mormons.

Gatlin served as adjutant of the post for part of his time at Fort Laramie, but he directed his attentions then, and later while at Fort Bridger, toward his new daughter. He wrote, "Susan was christened at Fort Laramie in July 1858 by the Rev. Mr. Vaux, Chaplain of the post, Major and Mrs. Lynde standing sponsors for her…Her first tooth made its appearance at Fort Laramie much to the delight of her mother, who has often acknowledged the pleasure she experienced in making the discovery."[146]

Major Isaac Lynde was a Vermont native who graduated from the U.S. Military Academy in 1827 and worked his way up the ranks with the Fifth Infantry, serving mainly in the Old Northwest. In 1855, he was promoted to major of the Seventh Infantry, and when the Seventh occupied Fort Laramie in 1857, he assumed command of that post. Major Lynde and Gatlin developed a close friendship during their stay at Fort Laramie.

Gatlin's travels were far from finished. After only a year at Fort Laramie, he was transferred again, this time even farther west to Utah Territory. While most of the army had gone to Utah—including nine of the ten companies of the Seventh Infantry, which was stationed with Colonel Albert Sidney Johnston at Camp Floyd, about 40 miles from Salt Lake City—Gatlin's Company F was assigned to Fort Bridger, some 130 miles northeast of Salt Lake. Explorers and traders Jim Bridger and Louis Vasquez had established Fort Bridger in 1843. It had been an important stop along the Oregon Trail, had been on the route of the Overland Stage and was to become a stop on the Pony Express during Gatlin's stay. When the Mormons occupied Utah, they bought the fort site from Bridger, and a thriving little community had built up around it. However, when word reached Brigham Young in 1857 that the U.S. Army was approaching, he ordered Fort Bridger to be burned and abandoned. The army took possession of the burned-out fort in August 1858 and established it as a permanent post. As part of the army's rebuilding effort, Gatlin's job was to supervise the erection of public buildings in and around the fort. Gatlin wrote of this transfer, "Remained in Garrison at Fort Laramie until 7th Augst '58 when we were relieved by the 4th Art., and proceeded with Co. to Utah, arrived at Fort Bridger 3rd Sept. and entered on duty as part of the garrison of that post. Did duty as a Adjunt. At Laramie from April to Augst '58 and at Fort Bridger from 1st Oct '58 to 31 Mar '59."[147]

Fort Bridger was a barren place when Gatlin and his family arrived. They were forced to live in tents the first few months, the coldest months of one of the coldest winters on record. Between his duties as post adjutant and superintendent of construction, Gatlin continued to delight in the company of his baby daughter, watching over her and attending to her needs as only a doting father can. Writing about Susan's experience at Fort Bridger, he also described the discomfort his family felt living in such a harsh environment:

Camp at Fort Bridger, Utah Territory, during Colonel Albert Johnston's Utah Expedition. From *Harper's Weekly*, January 30, 1858. *Library of Congress.*

> *Her experience in camp life commenced Aug 7th 1858, her father having taken her mother and herself with him when ordered with his company to Fort Bridger Utah Territory. This was a long march of over four hundred miles and was not completed until about the 3rd of Septr. At Fort Bridger they continued in tents until the 10th Jany '59 when the quarters were sufficiently finished for occupation. During periods of tent life the cold was extreme even for that climate, the thermometer being as low as 28° below zero at 7 o'clock A.M. on one occasion. Twice she had the bad luck to kick herself out of bed during this cold weather, but as she cried sharply on both occasions she soon woke her father who restored her to her warm bed, where she soon fell asleep and experienced no inconvenience from her cold bath.*[148]

Both Gatlin's family and his servant's family continued to grow at Fort Bridger, as evidenced by Gatlin's February 27, 1860 letter to his sister Mary in California:

> *The 22nd inst* [Washington's birthday] *was a great day for the nation at large, and doubly so for me individually, for at 7:30 a.m. on that day, a fine boy was born who is to be the representative of our house...I dare not presume that he will equal Johnny, but I hope he will resemble him as near as possible...We are all looking anxiously for the orders...that will take us out of Utah...We started from Fort Smith in August '57 with five, now we number eight...Prov's boy George is a nice looking fellow but is not healthy.*[149]

The Gatlins named their new son Richard Caswell Gatlin Jr. At age forty-nine, Gatlin appeared to focus more on family matters than on military affairs as he lavished love and attention on his two young children. For his family's sake, due to the harshness and isolation of Utah's mountains, leaving Fort Bridger became a priority for him.

The anticipated orders to leave Utah did finally come. Since the close of the Mexican War and the acquisition of the New Mexico Territory, the United States government had done nearly constant battle with the Apache and Navajo Indians in that territory. Gatlin's former Seventh Infantry mates Benjamin L.E. Bonneville and Dixon S. Miles had led offensive campaigns against the Navajos in 1857 and 1858, respectively, without conquering them. In early 1860, repeated hostilities between the whites and the Navajos around Fort Craig, New Mexico, attracted serious attention in Washington. Colonel Pitcairn Morrison was dispatched from Utah, along with the entire Seventh Infantry, to New Mexico on June 8, 1860. After packing their belongings and ample provisions in a wagon, Gatlin and his family and servants left Fort Bridger on June 4 bound for New Mexico. In his papers, Gatlin wrote:

> *Remained in garrison at Fort Bridger until 4 June '60, when company joined 2nd Sub column, Maj. Lynde Comdg. Column marched for New Mex June 8th taking the Bridgers Pass, Cheyenne Pass and Saugra de Christi Pass route. Arrived at Santa Fe Augst., when the column was broken up and Cos. D, F, K 7th Inf. ordered Ft. Craig where they arrived on the 30th Augst under my command.*[150]

Again writing for his daughter Susan's benefit, and showing a tendency to be more animated when referring to his family than when expounding on his military duties, Gatlin further described the arduous journey from Utah to New Mexico:

> *Early in June 1860, her father being ordered with his company to New Mexico took her and her mother and Richard into camp and here commenced her second experience of camp life. This march was quite a long one, lasting to the end of August when they all arrived safely at Fort Craig. On this march she rode in a wagon with her mother, brother and their servants Caroline and Sally as far as Santa Fe when a carriage was purchased. They must have had a nice time sleeping in that wagon, for the march always commenced so early in the morning that they never fairly awoke before she was put into it with the basket of provisions to which ample justice was done during the day. Nothing happened to her of official note on this march. Except that at Fernando del Taos she received her first India rubber toy, a Goddess of Liberty.*[151]

Upon arriving in Santa Fe in August 1860, the army dispersed to forts in New Mexico and to what would later become Arizona. Gatlin commanded three companies at Fort Craig. Located far up the Rio Grande nearly in the middle of New Mexico Territory, Fort Craig had been the scene of recent Navajo incursions. With Gatlin at Fort Craig, and under his command, were future Confederate generals Captain LaFayette McLaws and Second Lieutenant Joseph Wheeler. Although Gatlin was the nominal commander at Fort Craig, he was absent from the post from September to November 1860 while serving on general court-martial duty at Fort Bliss, Texas. He returned to Fort Craig about the time of the presidential election of 1860.[152] New Mexico was Navajo and Apache country, and the army's job was to keep a tenuous peace with the likes of Cochise, an Apache chief. Yet nothing the army could do would keep a peace, tenuous or otherwise, between the states of the South and those of the North. The election of Republican Abraham Lincoln ensured that.

In December 1860, in response to Lincoln's election, South Carolina left the Union. Mississippi, Florida, Alabama, Georgia and Louisiana followed in January, and Texas followed in February. Army and navy officers from those states faced a tremendously perplexing crisis of loyalty. Although they served the Federal government, their home states were no longer part of that government. They were sworn to defend the Union; however, although the Union was not yet at war with the seceded states, could they do so against their own people? Additionally, if they left the army or navy to serve with the Confederacy, they would find themselves lining up against old friends and comrades who had remained with the Union. Some officers from the remaining slave states, including Gatlin, hoped against hope that their states would remain in the Union and that peace could be maintained.[153]

In New Mexico, the situation was especially tense because the nearest army supply posts in Texas and Louisiana had fallen into Confederate hands, and several of the Federal officers at those posts were now in the Confederate service.[154] In Texas, General David Twiggs, who in 1832 had directed the return of Gatlin, the West Pointers and two of Winfield Scott's cholera-stricken steamers back to Buffalo from the Black Hawk War, handed over to the Confederacy, without a fight, virtually all the Federal government's military facilities and troops based in the Lone Star State.

Deeply troubled by this turn of events, and because Mary Ann had not seen her mother in nearly three years, Gatlin decided to take a sixty-day furlough to visit Fort Smith. He and his family set out across New Mexico and Texas by wagon, stopping at Indianola, Texas, to inform the Texas authorities, who were now part of the Confederate States, of his intentions. From Indianola, he sent a note to the assistant adjutant general of Texas that said in part: "I arrived at this place…from Fort Craig, New Mexico bringing with me Privates Gibrey and Keim of 'F' Co. 7th Inf. Designing to send them back with the public wagon and team used in transporting my baggage."[155]

Gatlin delighted in traveling with his family. He was especially fond of describing events from little Susan's perspective and did so when he wrote about their journey to Fort Smith:

> *She remained at Fort Craig until 6th Feby 1861 when she accompanied her parents on a visit to her grandmother at Fort Smith. This was a long and tedious journey. They were compelled to travel with an escort of troops and to encamp every night except when reaching a military post on the route. This route passed Forts Fillmore, Bliss, Quitman, Davis, Comanche Springs and so on to San Antonio, Victoria and to the Gulf at Powder Horn which was reached about the 15th of March. Here the party took steamer for Berwick Bay, basing for a short time in Galveston. From the Bay by rail to New Orleans. At New Orleans, where we spent several days, she added largely to her stock of toys and made many additions to her wardrobe. Embarking on board the steamer* Arkansas *party reached Fort Smith on the 6th of April.*[156]

During the trip to Arkansas, Gatlin was promoted to full major effective February 26 and was transferred to the Fifth Infantry,[157] but he would never actively serve in his new capacity. One week after his arrival at Fort Smith, the

Confederate artillery under General P.G.T. Beauregard in South Carolina bombarded the small Federal garrison at Fort Sumter in Charleston Harbor. President Lincoln responded on April 15 by calling for volunteer troops from the remaining states to put down the rebellion. Lincoln also ordered various army officers to secure certain sites across the country. One of these officers was Gatlin, whom Lincoln ordered to secure the post at Fort Smith and to take command of Federal troops in Arkansas.[158]

When Gatlin arrived at Fort Smith, the northern tier of Southern states—Virginia, North Carolina, Tennessee and Arkansas—were still in the Union but were on the brink of seceding. In Arkansas, mixed loyalties between North and South existed. The people of northwestern Arkansas, including those of Fort Smith, were predominantly Union in sentiment. Secessionists ran the state government in Little Rock, however, and in April, the state commandeered the military facilities in all of Arkansas, including the post at Fort Smith.

On April 23, 1861, Gatlin joined Captain Alexander Montgomery at the post at Fort Smith just as the Federal garrison was abandoning it. The Federal First Cavalry under Captain S.D. Sturgis retreated en masse from the fort and rode southward for Fort Towson just hours before Arkansas secessionists ordered out by Governor Elias Rector landed from the Arkansas River and took possession of Fort Smith. Gatlin and Montgomery, realizing they could do nothing to keep the insurgents from their goal, acquiesced to being taken prisoner by the secessionists. After a brief negotiation with Colonel Solon Borland, leader of the Rebels, Gatlin and Montgomery secured a parole by promising not to bear arms against the State of Arkansas or against the new Confederate government. Gatlin seemed annoyed that the State of Arkansas would occupy a Federal fort prior to seceding from the Union. He was correct, however, in predicting that Arkansas would leave the Union in just a few days' time.[159]

Virginia seceded on April 17, 1861; Arkansas and Tennessee on May 6, 1861; and Gatlin's own North Carolina on May 20, 1861, the last of the eleven states to leave the Union. A slim majority of North Carolinians were decidedly pro-Union, and many of the state's leaders had hoped to avoid secession. But after Fort Sumter, when President Lincoln called on Governor Ellis for volunteers to help put down the Southern rebellion, Ellis spoke for the entire state by advising the president that he would not turn on his Southern brothers and would not provide any troops from North Carolina. Provoked by Lincoln's call for troops and by the secession of all its neighboring states, North Carolina had little choice but to secede. A state convention was called in May to decide the issue, and its delegates, many of whom had once been lukewarm to leaving the Union, opted for secession.

Despite his being a slave owner and a son of the plantation aristocracy, the idea of leaving the Union gave Gatlin serious misgivings. He viewed secession as revolution. Many of his friends, ex-governors William A. Graham and David Swain among them, were afraid that disunion would bring nothing but ruin to North Carolina, and Gatlin undoubtedly had the same fear. He was troubled that by joining the Confederate cause he would be taking up arms against some of his closest friends and allies, including Daniel Whiting, Isaac Lynde and Napoleon Dana. However, the same would be true if he stayed in the army. Most of his Southern peers were opting out of Federal service in homage to their home states. Already, T.H. Holmes, Gabriel Rains, LaFayette McLaws, Robert E. Lee, Earl Van Dorn, Joe Wheeler, Daniel Ruggles and many other of Gatlin's friends and fellow officers had resigned the army and been commissioned in their states' or Confederate services.

The issue ultimately was a matter of personal honor with Gatlin. He had made his decision even before the capture of Fort Smith and before North Carolina seceded. He could not bear arms, in good conscience, against the people of his home state. On the day the North Carolina Convention delegates voted to secede, May 20, 1861, after twenty-nine years in faithful Federal service, Gatlin submitted his letter of resignation to the adjutant general of the army. A few days later, he hastened to Raleigh to accept a commission in the North Carolina militia, leaving his small family at Fort Smith. In Gatlin's words:

> *Soon after my arrival at Fort Smith Arks from New Mexico on the 5th April 1861, becoming satisfied that most of the Southern states would soon be forced to take part in the revolution already commenced, I wrote to the Governor of No. Carolina tendering my services should the state secede from the United States. Having received from the Governor an invitation to repair to N.C., I resigned my commission of Major in the 5th Infy Army of the United States on the 20th of May 1861 and set out for Raleigh, where I arrived early in June.*[160]

Chapter 10

"The Undersigned Hereby Assumes Command": North Carolina Coastal Commander

With the certainty of war looming, North Carolina's government hastened in April and May 1861 to prepare. Although North Carolina had not yet left the Union, Governor John W. Ellis ordered state troops to secure Federal forts, the arsenal at Fayetteville and the mint at Charlotte, which they did. State adjutant general John F. Hoke began raising, arming and training volunteer regiments to be sent to Virginia. Ellis acquired the services of engineer Colonel William H.C. Whiting, recently responsible for constructing defensive works at Charleston, to develop a defensive plan for Wilmington and the southern North Carolina coast. Whiting deftly planned and began building batteries along the Cape Fear inlet.[161]

When, on May 20, 1861, the Secession Convention delegates took North Carolina out of the Union, North Carolina became the last state to leave the Union and the next to last to join the Confederacy, Tennessee having already seceded but not yet having allied itself with the Confederacy. Weak sentiment existed among some of the delegates, especially former governor William A. Graham, for North Carolina to forego the Confederacy and remain a free and independent state. The convention members, however, voted by unanimous acclamation to ally North Carolina with the Confederacy, although the final adoption of the Confederate Constitution was not accomplished until June 6, 1861. The convention members also provided for a military board and appointed state representative Warren Winslow secretary of military affairs.

The excited transition from peacetime North Carolina to wartime North Carolina lost important momentum when, on May 23, 1861, Whiting tendered his resignation after only a month on the job. Whiting had been in complete charge of coastal operations but bypassed Ellis's authority on one occasion by ordering iron directly from Virginia. An irate Ellis, perhaps as a slight to Whiting, appointed Brigadier General Theophilus H. Holmes to command the militia troops on the coast. Whiting, thus subordinated to Holmes, soon resigned, perhaps with resentment, to take other duties in Virginia. The loss of Whiting left an engineering void that slowed North Carolina's defensive preparations by several weeks.[162]

On May 27, one week into secession, the military board formally divided the coast into two administrative departments. The Northern Coastal Department encompassed that area from New River in Onslow County to the

Top: John Ellis, the first of North Carolina's three Civil War governors. *North Carolina Archives*.

Right: Major General William H.C. Whiting designed North Carolina's southern coast defenses. *Wikimedia Commons*.

Virginia border, and newly appointed state brigadier general Walter Gwynn, recently arrived in North Carolina after duty as Virginia's militia commander of the Norfolk area, assumed command. Gwynn established his headquarters in New Bern and began immediately inspecting his domain. Under Gwynn's direction, work progressed steadily in the Northern Coastal District with new forts at Hatteras Inlet, Roanoke Island and other key places along the Outer Banks, as well as at New Bern.[163]

Brigadier General T.H. Holmes, who had been, since late April, already commanding coastal militia troops and overseeing construction of defensive works in Wilmington, took command of the Southern Coastal Department, which ran from the New River to the South Carolina border. Holmes, who had resigned his U.S. Army commission on April 5, 1861, to join the North Carolina State Militia, did not remain in command for long, however. Within a week of his May 27, 1861 appointment, he accepted the commission as brigadier general in the Provisional Confederate Army offered by his good friend and West Point classmate President Jefferson Davis and departed North Carolina to lead a brigade in Fredericksburg, Virginia. Replacing Holmes as commander of the Southern Coast defenses on an interim basis was Colonel Charles C. Tew, who had been commanding the Twelfth North Carolina Volunteer Regiment at Fort Macon on Bogue Banks near Beaufort. Further work in Wilmington would wait until the Southern Coast Defense command structure solidified.[164]

When Gatlin arrived in Raleigh in early June, Governor Ellis appointed him commander of North Carolina's Southern Coastal Defenses with the rank of brigadier general of state troops, replacing Colonel Tew. Gatlin proceeded to Wilmington; assumed his post on June 22, 1861; and continued directing the construction of the defensive works begun earlier by Whiting. He acknowledged his appointment with the following dispatch, probably excited and gratified to be able to write under his name the title "brigadier general":

> *Pursuant to paragraph 6 of General Orders, Numbers 4. from the Adjutant-General's Office, dated at Raleigh, N.C. June 18, 1861, the undersigned hereby assumes command of this department. All communication for these headquarters from persons under my command will be addressed to Lieutenant Colonel Richard H. Riddick, assistant adjutant-general, who has been assigned to duty in this department by paragraph 7 of the same general orders.*[165]

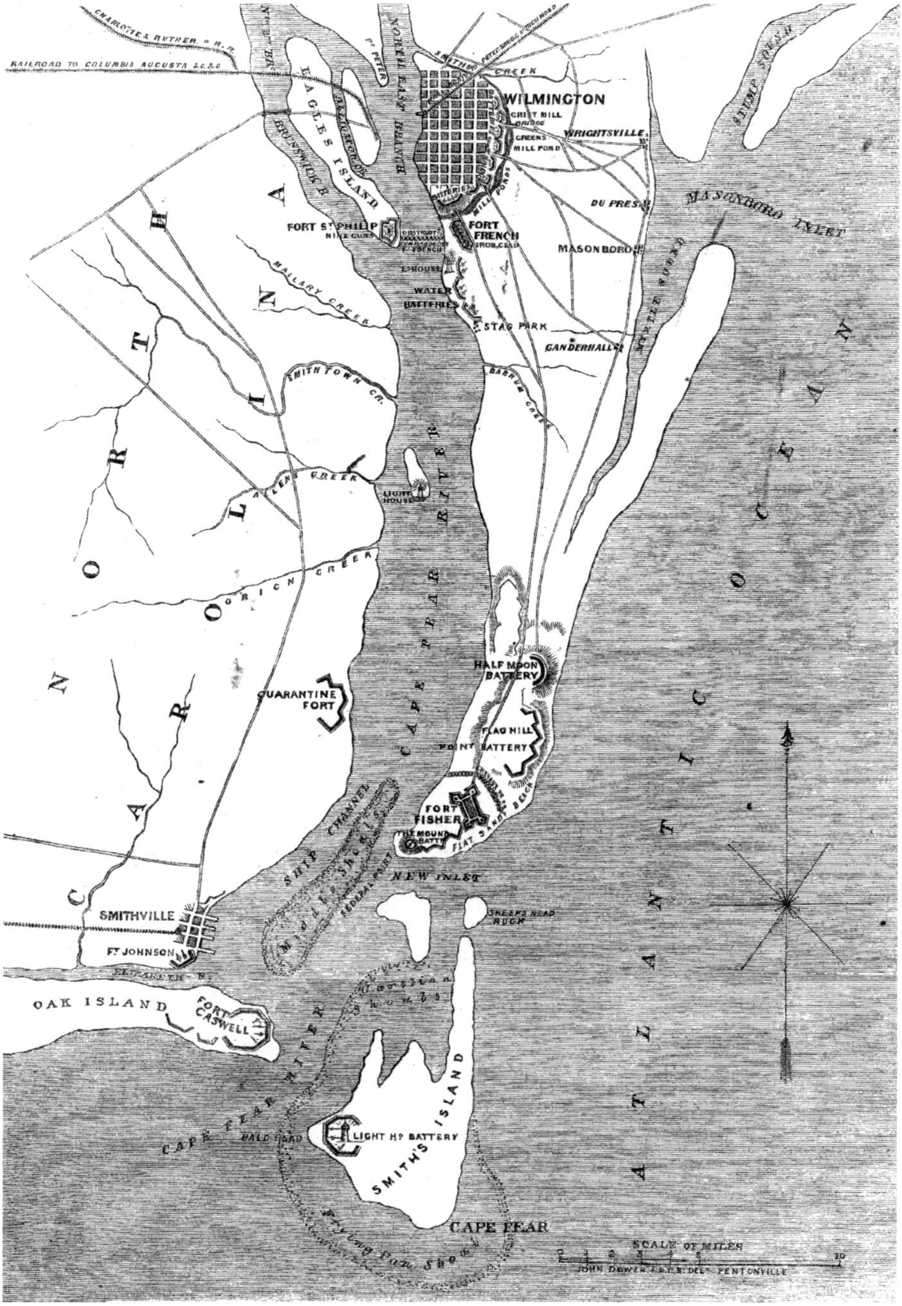

Cape Fear River and the approaches to Wilmington early in the war. *North Carolina Archives.*

On June 10, 1861, events reached a point of no return when eight hundred recruits of the First North Carolina Volunteers under Colonel Daniel Harvey Hill, assisted by some six hundred men from Virginia companies of infantry, artillery and cavalry, drove off a larger Yankee force under General Benjamin Butler at Big Bethel near Yorktown, Virginia, in the first significant land battle of the Civil War. Hill's regiment had been formed in April and, with minimal training, sent to Virginia on May 21 in the vanguard of troops sent by Governor Ellis to Virginia. The only Southern fatality, Private Henry Wyatt of Edgecombe County, North Carolina, was the first Confederate killed in the war. Six weeks later, on July 21, 1861, North Carolinian T.H. Holmes figured prominently in the first Battle of Manassas, or First Bull Run, a second major Confederate victory in Virginia. During that early summer, the war appeared to be going the way of the Confederacy, although the fighting was confined mostly to Virginia.

Meanwhile, on the Pamlico and Albemarle Sounds in North Carolina's Northern Coast District, Brigadier General Gwynn continued busily fortifying Hatteras Inlet, Roanoke Island, New Bern and a few other key points along the central and northern coasts. Gwynn had graduated from the United States Military Academy in 1825 but had not served on active duty since 1832. He was a respected engineer, however, and upon joining the Virginia militia in April 1861 was chosen by Governor Letcher of Virginia to command the Norfolk Division. When the Confederate government moved to Richmond on May 21, the commander of the Confederate forces in Virginia, General P.G.T. Beauregard, found the Norfolk Department in disarray and persuaded President Davis to replace Gwynn at Norfolk with Brigadier General Benjamin Huger from South Carolina. Gwynn quickly resurfaced in North Carolina, where, during June and July, he made critical assessments of the defensive needs of the coast. He first visited Fort Macon in late May and began arranging for labor and the much-needed addition of heavy cannon. On June 6, 1861, he pointed out to Governor Ellis the pressing need for the state to organize its engineering and ordnance departments efficiently, noting that, in serving as his own engineer, his administrative objectives were suffering. Gwynn's assessment of the entire coast was that it could not be defended "without mounted artillery and cavalry."[166] In an eleven-point report to Governor Clark on July 22, 1861, Gwynn warned of the danger to Hatteras if new companies to replace the twelve-month enlistees of the Seventh North Carolina Volunteers and artillery units could not be formed and a regiment organized for the Outer Banks by the following month. He pleaded that failure to replace the twelve-month troops "would leave the batteries, now inadequately defended, at the mercy of the enemy."[167] He also sternly reminded the governor that his month-old requisition for "stores of every description" for Hatteras had yet to be fulfilled. Gwynn's report was an early alarm that perhaps the coast of North Carolina would not, or could not, be secured. Despite Gwynn's expert planning and his insightful analysis, his task was too daunting for one man—he was stretched too thin. The area of his command was so vast, over two hundred miles long by water and far more by land, from New River in Onslow County to the Virginia border, that he could not inspect his entire command in any kind of timely manner. The distance and difficulty of travel along the central and northern North Carolina coast were much too intense to be accomplished effectively by one commander. Gwynn, realizing this, advised the military board secretary, Warren Winslow, that his area could be better defended if divided into two departments, each with its own commander.

Meanwhile, in the Southern Coastal Department, Gatlin had fewer difficulties—at least in terms of travel. He continued directing the development of the partially completed batteries and forts around Wilmington, including what would eventually become Fort Fisher, according to plans drawn by engineer W.H.C. Whiting. Gatlin met frequently with Wilmington's local officials and leading citizens. In late June, he was called on by LaFayette McLaws, a former subordinate officer from the Seventh Infantry. Recently appointed colonel of the Tenth Georgia Infantry, McLaws stopped in Wilmington to pay his respects while en route to join his regiment in Virginia. General Gatlin was extremely busy, according to McLaws, so their meeting was brief, but McLaws was gratified to see his former commanding officer wearing the general's insignia of North Carolina.[168]

Governor Ellis had unceasingly directed North Carolina's military buildup during the spring and early summer of 1861 despite being seriously unwell. By late June, he was so weak that he was compelled to seek the curative air of Red Sulphur Springs, Virginia. His hopes for a recovery did not materialize. Governor Ellis died on July 7 of tuberculosis while still in Virginia. Speaker of the House Henry Toole Clark, of Tarboro, succeeded Ellis as governor in accordance with the state's succession rules and immediately inherited what proved to be a debilitating turn of events. On June 27, 1861, ten days prior to Ellis's death, the military board had announced that North Carolina's defenses would be assumed by the Confederate War Department effective August 20, 1861. That appeared to be good news for the state's war effort, but in anticipation of the Confederacy's assuming responsibility, the military board immediately suspended all state military expenditures. A month earlier, the board had also rejected a suggestion from concerned Halifax County citizens that the state raise and dedicate seven regiments of its own to man and protect the North Carolina coastline. The board's confidence was vested instead in the Confederacy.[169]

The sudden lack of funding barely slowed Gwynn's work at Fort Macon, where soldiers and impressed slaves cleared the surrounding beaches of brush and trees and mounted heavy cannon. However, the defunding forced a halt to the construction of defensive works around Wilmington, where the state-hired engineers and workers were dismissed or assigned elsewhere. The resulting inactivity robbed North Carolina of valuable time, and an alarmed Gatlin let Clark know it. Surveying the defenses at Wilmington following the state's cessation of financial support, and recognizing the urgency of the situation, Gatlin optimistically reported to Secretary Winslow his plan for the state to complete the work at Wilmington if the Confederacy would pay for it:

> *HDQRS. SOUTHERN DEPARTMENT, COAST DEFENSES,*
> *Wilmington, N.C., July 17, 1861.*
> *Honorable WARREN WINSLOW,*
> *Secretary of Military Affairs, Raleigh, N.C.:*
>
> *SIR:*
>
> *I shall be glad to receive the eleven 32-pounders, but the order to discontinue expenditures on account of the State will prevent their immediate use, as the batteries for which they were required have not been erected. Three of the batteries erected by General Whiting were not commenced when the engineer and his laborers were discharged. Besides these, two other batteries should be erected on the coast above Confederate Point Light, and this without delay. In order that you may understand the importance of these contemplated batteries I will explain. New Inlet is protected, one at Zeek's Island and the other at Confederate Point, on the opposite side of the channel. To prevent this latter from being turned by an enemy landing on the main I have established a camp for the Eighth Regiment of Volunteers near the head of the sound, about five miles from the light, and which is called Camp Wyatt. These troops are further intended to march against the enemy, should he land upon the banks; but as in that case to reach the mainland he would have to cross the sound it is not likely to be attempted. The coast for fifteen miles above Confederate Point offers great facilities for landing. In ordinary*

weather, and when the wind is westerly, the sea is smooth and there is little or no surf, while there are three fathoms of water within half a mile of the shore. By erecting a battery near Camp Wyatt and another some two miles and a half nearer Confederate Point, the vessels of the enemy would be compelled to keep at least two miles from shore, and his landing would be rendered difficult, if not impossible. As it now stands he could run near enough to Camp Wyatt to fire a broadside into it. I hope you will agree with me that these two batteries ought to be erected at once. Should it be determined to do so, I must request that Captain Winder, who is now on recruiting service under the orders of Colonel Bradford, be directed to return here and resume the duties of chief engineer.

Very respectfully, your obedient servant,

R.C. GATLIN,
Brigadier-General, Commanding[170]

Complementing Whiting's earlier plans, Gatlin established and garrisoned Camp Wyatt on the Cape Fear River about fifteen miles north of the entrance to New Inlet. He proposed adding two additional artillery batteries on the Atlantic Ocean, one near present-day Carolina Beach and the other a few miles farther south at present-day Kure Beach. Winslow forwarded Gatlin's letter to the Confederate War Department, which, in turn, responded in early August to Governor Clark that Gatlin's plan was a good one and that funds to accomplish it were forthcoming.[171]

In the meantime, Gatlin was obliged to respond, on July 23, 1861, to a committee of concerned Wilmington citizens that because all state expenditures for defensive works had been suspended, he had issued orders "directing all work to cease on the forts and batteries in this harbor and along the coast and the laborers discharged."[172] When assurances of Confederate funding for completing Wilmington's defensive works arrived, the result of Gatlin's urging, the work was continued, and the batteries that Gatlin suggested were eventually completed, but no additional works were started for lack of funding. Gatlin's new batteries were eventually named Battery Gatlin and Battery Anderson. Gatlin also secured the services of another Confederate engineer, Captain John T. Winder, to assist the chief engineer, Sewell L. Fremont, who was a colonel in state service. In July and August, Gatlin was cautiously optimistic that the defenses established around Wilmington and elsewhere would, with the creation of a naval force to protect the sounds and rivers, be adequate to repulse any Union attempt to land on Tar Heel soil. That optimism would ultimately be shattered, although the defenses at Wilmington did prove sufficient to keep the Union navy far enough off shore for that port to remain open until nearly the end of the war.

The whirlwind of Civil War was not confined to the East. Back in New Mexico, which only five months earlier had been the scene of Gatlin's Fort Craig command, a wavering and uncertain Federal army was taunted and terrorized by the confident new Confederates from Texas. Gatlin learned that in late July, his own former Seventh Infantry Regiment, under command of his good friend Major Isaac Lynde, while attempting a disorganized retreat to join other Union regiments, had ignominiously surrendered without firing a shot to a much smaller Confederate battalion at San Augustine Springs. In that New Mexico desert, seven hundred thirsty and exhausted Union soldiers became prisoners of war, southern New Mexico fell under Confederate control and the North had yet another major embarrassment to shoulder along with losses at Big Bethel and Manassas. For his part, the Northern press excoriated Major Lynde as a coward and a traitor. As a result, despite his later exoneration by General Grant, Lynde's reputation and career were ruined. Lynde and his wife had stood up for Gatlin's daughter at her christening at Fort Laramie less than four years earlier, and Gatlin had been with Lynde's column that marched from Utah to New Mexico in 1860. Gatlin could not have been disappointed by the Confederate victory, but it is likely that he felt sincere regret that his good friend Lynde, a noble soldier and his former commander, had fallen into such disgrace. Gatlin had no way of knowing that, eight months later, he himself would be subjected to similar intense public vitriol.

Little of note happened on the North Carolina coast during the month and a half leading to the Confederate takeover. In late July, engineer Colonel W. Beverhout Thompson reported that the two new forts at Hatteras Inlet were complete and sufficiently armed to prevent any naval incursion through the inlet. He warned, however, that additional troops would be needed to repel a land invasion. Having inspected his entire command, General Gwynn was satisfied that, given the lack of rifled cannon and supporting troops, New Bern and Fort Macon had been made as impenetrable as possible.

Finally, on August 19, 1861, Gatlin received a telegram from General Samuel Cooper, adjutant general of the Confederacy, informing him that he had been appointed to the rank of brigadier general in the Provisional Army of the Confederate States and had been assigned to command the Confederacy's newly created North Carolina Department.[173] This marked the transfer of North Carolina troops and coastal defenses to the Confederacy. Except for certain twelve-month enlistees, the North Carolina State Troops were mustered into the Provisional Confederate Army. Gatlin did not acknowledge and accept his appointment until August 25, 1861, even though Special Order Number 130 had been issued from the Confederate adjutant general's office on August 21, 1861, making Gatlin's appointment official. Gatlin, who had initially sought merely to serve his state, no longer served under direction of Governor Clark and the North Carolina Military Board. He now served as one of Jefferson Davis's Confederate generals. Of his experience as commander of the Southern Coastal Defenses, Gatlin tersely wrote:

> *On the 18th of June 1861, I was appointed Brigadier General in the State Forces and ordered to the command of the Southern Department of the Coast Defenses. I proceeded at once to Wilmington and assumed command. The defensive works there in progress were continued to completion, but no others were undertaken in as much as the Governor directed early in July that all executions on account of engineering and ordinance should cease, the Convention having resolved to turn over the military establishment of the state to the Confederate government. Little else was done other than to complete the organization of the 18th and 20th Regiments to dispose of them to the best advantage and to see that they were prepared for service as speedily as possible. The forces under my command were Moore's Battery, Edmunston's Company of cavalry, and the two Regmts above referred to. I continued in this command until the 26th of August, on which day the forces of the state were turned over to the Confederate government.*[174]

On August 20, 1861, Gatlin and Clark were cautiously optimistic that the Confederacy would provide North Carolina with more abundant resources and stronger and more effective war management than the state could on its own. No one knew it then, but the Confederate War Department and Jefferson Davis would prove to be masters of neglect, mismanagement and dereliction in the matter of the North Carolina war effort.

Chapter 11

"These Defenses Have Been Too Long Neglected": Yankee Invasion

With the Confederate takeover, North Carolina's coast defense departments merged into the single Confederate Department of North Carolina with General Gatlin as department commander. Gatlin was the ranking Confederate officer in the state. He no longer reported to Governor Clark but to Confederate adjutant general Samuel Cooper, who, in turn, reported to the head of the Confederate War Department, Secretary of War LeRoy Walker. Gatlin typically directed correspondence to Cooper, but correspondence from the War Department could come from Secretary Walker, from Adjutant General Cooper or from the assistant adjutant general. Governor Clark no longer directed the military operations in his state, and the state military board shut down. Clark did remain responsible for recruiting, clothing, equipping and training new regiments of North Carolina soldiers for enrollment into Confederate service. For this, he relied on Adjutant General James G. Martin, who also commanded the state militia.[175]

Gatlin's new responsibilities, in addition to administering the department, were to deploy the troops assigned by the War Department to North Carolina and to direct the fortification of the state's strategic points. The Confederate War Department, along with President Davis, was responsible for devising strategy and for arming, feeding and paying the troops. Unfortunately for Gatlin and for North Carolina, General Gwynn, who had done much to strengthen North Carolina's coastline, did not remain in North Carolina as a commander or even as an engineer. He returned to Richmond to serve in the Confederate adjutant general's department and mustered in as a colonel in the Provisional Confederate Army.[176]

Upon assuming his new command, General Gatlin's first order of business was to establish his permanent departmental headquarters. Gatlin opted to do that at the strategically situated town of Goldsboro, a town of fewer than two thousand residents but located in the middle of North Carolina's coastal plain, within easy traveling distance by rail of Raleigh, New Bern and Wilmington. Goldsboro was the point of intersection of the Wilmington & Weldon Railroad that ran north and south, the North Carolina Railroad that ran east and west from Charlotte to Goldsboro and the Atlantic and North Carolina Railroad that ran east and west from Goldsboro to the coast. By placing his headquarters near that junction, Gatlin would have easy rail access for himself and his staff, as well as for reserve troops, which he could quickly deploy to the coast if needed. Making Goldsboro even more desirable was the presence of Gatlin's half sister, Ann Hooks, who lived in the prosperous little town of Everettsville, just five miles by rail south of Goldsboro. Ann's husband, the Reverend Curtis Hooks, had died in 1855, leaving her a large house and lot. The house was suitable for Gatlin's family and offered Ann Hooks the opportunity to become well acquainted with Mary Ann, Susie and little Dick Gatlin when they arrived from Arkansas. Gatlin planned to meet his family in Memphis and escort them to their new home as soon as he established his new headquarters.

Wrapping up his business in Wilmington, Gatlin reiterated the urgency of securing the defenses of the southern coast by requesting from Governor Clark the services of Sewell L. Fremont as a full-time engineer to oversee and improve the works in the Cape Fear area. In an effort to have his engineer join the Confederate payroll, Gatlin wrote to Adjutant General Cooper:

> *Colonel S.L. Fremont, First Regiment Artillery North Carolina Militia, has, by direction of Governor Clark, reported to me for duty. It is desirable to have his services as chief engineer of the defenses of the Cape Fear and the neighboring coast, and I respectfully request authority to muster him into the service of the Confederate States with that view. These defenses have been too long neglected; no time should be lost in resuming the works.*[177]

However, before departing Wilmington for Goldsboro, Gatlin received word from General Huger, on August 27, 1861, that a Federal fleet had left Hampton Roads en route for the North Carolina coast.[178] Gatlin quickly wired

Union general Benjamin Butler commanded the attack and capture of Hatteras Inlet in August 1861. *Library of Congress.*

Governor Clark to send all available troops to Goldsboro until it could be determined where the fleet intended to attack, possibly Wilmington, New Bern or the Outer Banks. On August 28, 1861, word reached Wilmington that the Federals had gathered at Hatteras Inlet. Gatlin then ordered all troops to rush from Goldsboro to New Bern, and he rode the rails to New Bern himself the next morning.[179]

Smarting from the recent losses at Big Bethel and Manassas, the Union army needed success on some front. The Union fleet, commanded jointly by Commodore Silas Stringham and General Benjamin Butler, pulled within sight of the Hatteras lighthouse on the morning of August 27, 1861. By mid-morning, 318 Federal infantrymen had landed on North Carolina's shore, and the Confederates guarding the Hatteras

Capture of the Confederate forts at Hatteras Inlet, August 27, 1861. *Library of Congress.*

Inlet found themselves under heavy artillery fire. The guns of the two unimposing sand and sod structures at Hatteras Inlet, Forts Clark and Hatteras, garrisoned by about 300 soldiers of the Seventh North Carolina Volunteers, could not match the range of the Union cannon, and the forts became sitting ducks. Fort Clark, more northerly and nearest to the Union fleet, took a heavy pounding from the Federal warships. When Fort Clark's ammunition ran out by 12:30 that afternoon, its garrison spiked its six thirty-two-pound cannons and retreated to Fort Hatteras. The Yankees, realizing their advantage, poured into Fort Clark, and the Stars and Stripes once again flew over North Carolina soil.[180]

Late that night, Commodore Samuel Barron and Confederate reinforcements arrived from the post at Portsmouth farther down the Outer Banks and added to the force at Fort Hatteras. By 7:30 on the morning of August 28, 1861, the Union bombardment resumed. Unable to match the range of the Union artillery from his Fort Hatteras stronghold, Commodore Barron surrendered the entire Confederate force, 580 men. Barron had more men at Fort Hatteras than Butler had at Fort Clark and might have won the victory had he shown more daring and counterattacked Fort Clark during the night. It is doubtful that Commodore Stringham would have shelled Fort Clark as long as Federal soldiers were in it, and without naval gunfire support, Butler's men likely would have retreated. Barron either did not realize his advantage or was too unsure to press it. As a result, the North gained its first significant victory of the war and ruled North Carolina soil at the Tar Heel State's most critical point of defense. The Confederates might have thwarted the Union landing had Forts Clark and Hatteras been properly outfitted with longer-range rifled guns and the 5,000 men recommended by General Gwynn and engineer Thompson, but the Confederate War Department was hard-pressed to arm the Confederate forts and troops in North Carolina—then and for the remainder of the war.

In New Bern, at just past midnight on August 30, 1861, Gatlin received the startling news that the Federals had captured Hatteras Inlet on the North Carolina Outer Banks. He quickly wired General Cooper in Richmond: "The forts at Hatteras, with the garrisons, numbering 580 men, also Commodore Barron and Colonel Bradford, were captured at 11.30 a.m. yesterday."[181] Gatlin did not sleep that night but gathered his things and what staff he had with him and caught the earliest train from New Bern to Goldsboro. From there, he again wired General Cooper with more details and with the first of many pleas for troops to defend his invaded state:

> *The steamer* Winslow, *just arrived here from Hatteras, Captain Sinclair, reports the forts there captured by the enemy at 11.30 Commodore Barron, Colonel Bradford, and the garrison, numbering about 580 men, including the field officers of Seventh Regiment of volunteers surrendered. I will make such arrangements as I can for present defense against further disaster. Please order General Huger to send four regiments and a light battery to the eastern counties, and a number of heavy guns with an engineer to fortify such points as may be necessary. I have only the Seventh Regiment of State troops at my disposal.*[182]

That the Confederacy and General Gatlin were surprised is certain. Gatlin, however, bore little to no blame for the defeat at Hatteras since he had been in command for only one week when the catastrophe occurred. If any blame was due to the forts being poorly armed and undermanned, it was difficult to pinpoint it. The forts' engineer, Beverhout Thompson, had warned that a troop buildup was mandatory, as had General Gwynn. Gwynn's former aide, R.R. Collier, reminded President Davis in a letter on August 30 that Gwynn had proposed far more troops at Hatteras than the Confederacy had provided.[183] Confederate officials were justifiably preoccupied with arming Virginia and had few resources to spare. Governor

Clark, of necessity, was compelled to marshal any few newly formed North Carolina regiments among the various potential Union targets in his state. In reality, with three hundred miles of North Carolina coastline to guard and so few resources with which to do it, it would have been difficult for anyone to accurately predict where the Federal force would strike, much less arm the targeted place to adequately repel an all-out attack.

Upon hearing of the disaster at Hatteras, Gatlin's old friend T.H. Holmes took the liberty of writing directly to Jefferson Davis, on August 31, 1861, regarding the situation in North Carolina:

> *BROOKE'S STATION, August 31, 1861.*
>
> *If Hatteras has fallen, the danger is incalculable, and as it shows the utter absence of commonest judgment and forethought, I tremble for its sequel, unless you will send a competent officer there to command. My excellent friend General Gatlin, though perfectly devoted and true of heart, is as ignorant as I was of the necessities of that important frontier, and there is no one there of military acumen with whom he can advise and consult. It is with the greatest diffidence that I make a suggestion to you, but I am obliged to think that the energy, science, and industry of General Whiting, together with his intimate acquaintance with the whole coast, point to him as the proper commander to guard against further injury in that quarter.*[184]

Holmes was by no means criticizing Gatlin. Rather, he was suggesting that the president send W.H.C. Whiting, who had the type of engineering skill set needed to manage the North Carolina coast defenses and who, in April 1861, had designed and built defensive batteries near Wilmington, to assist or direct Gatlin.

Governor Clark's August 30, 1861 report to Adjutant General Cooper signals the precariousness of North Carolina's defensive strength. The department's troops included "Two regiments at mouth of Cape Fear, five companies at Fort Macon, one regiment captured at Hatteras, one regiment and two battalions at New Berne. A light battery at New Berne, but no ammunition. Two regiments organizing here, ready to move in two or three days. Any number of volunteers offering, but very scarce of arms."[185] Days later, Gatlin reported a somewhat improved picture of his department's troop strength, but the forces in his department were still meager. In early September, the Eighteenth and Twentieth North Carolina Regiments and a company of cavalry were at Wilmington. Singletary's infantry battalion

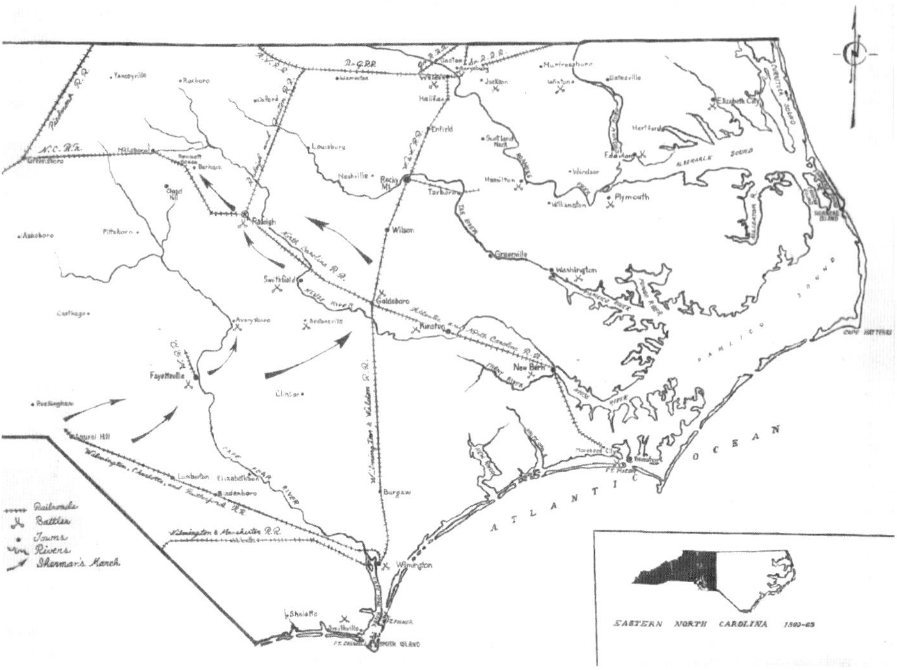

A map of eastern North Carolina (1860–65) showing Goldsboro as the junction of the state's three major railroads. *North Carolina Archives*.

(later the Twenty-seventh North Carolina Regiment) and two artillery batteries were at New Bern. The Seventh and Twenty-sixth Regiments were on Bogue Banks. Three companies of infantry and four companies of artillery were at Fort Macon. Two companies of the Seventeenth Regiment were at Washington. The Third Georgia Regiment and a detachment of the Seventeenth Regiment guarded Roanoke Island. A battery and two regiments were forming at Raleigh. The Twenty-fifth Regiment was days away at Asheville. Gatlin implored of General Cooper on August 30, "Owing to the capture of Hatteras it is very necessary to fortify the rivers running into the [Pamlico] sound. Have no disposable officer for that duty. Please send immediately a good engineer."[186] Over and again, to the point of redundancy in the coming months, Clark appealed for arms and Gatlin voiced the need for Confederate troops in eastern North Carolina.

Organizational challenges weighed on Gatlin from the moment he assumed command of the Department of North Carolina. The state's coast was long and broken but encompassed three distinct geographic sections. The Albemarle Sound region ran from the Virginia border to just south of Roanoke Island. The Pasquotank, Chowan, Roanoke and Alligator Rivers emptied into the Albemarle Sound. The Pamlico Sound region was in the central part of the coast, surrounding the town of New Bern and through which drained the Pamlico, Neuse, White Oak and New Rivers. The Cape Fear region ran from the New River southward to the South Carolina border, surrounded the Cape Fear River and was the location of North Carolina's lifeline—the deepwater port at Wilmington. Access to the Albemarle and Pamlico Sound regions accrued to the Union when Hatteras Inlet fell in August. Gatlin's hope was to keep the Yankees bottled up on the Outer Banks by denying them access to the inland. As Gatlin stressed to the War Department, the success of this strategy depended on a strong presence of the Confederate navy with a sufficient number of gunboats to guard the river entrances. Protecting Roanoke Island by arming it with effective batteries was critical, for if Union forces controlled that key island, they could dominate all naval activity in both the Albemarle and Pamlico Sounds. Just as critical was keeping the port at Wilmington open because the blockade running through it provided North Carolina with much of the manufactured foreign goods and supplies that it and the Confederate government needed to carry on the war. Clark and Gatlin were in accord in petitioning the Confederate War Department for gunboats, heavy artillery, experienced military commanders and large numbers of well-armed troops to patrol each of the three regions. Militarily, Gatlin's strategy was by the book and sound in theory, but it was dependent on the Confederate War Department's ability to provide the prescribed resources. Optimism existed this early in the war that the War Department could deliver.

Chapter 12

"It Is to Be Regretted That General Hill Should Have Been Removed": Counting on the Confederacy

September 1861 was to be a month of false alarms and frustrating preparation in eastern North Carolina. A flurry of administrative activity in Richmond, Raleigh and Goldsboro followed the Hatteras debacle. Now that the Union army occupied Hatteras Inlet and controlled the central and northern North Carolina coastlines, a very real danger of the Federals moving upriver from the Pamlico Sound inland to New Bern, Washington, Greenville and Plymouth existed. Hoping to seal off the inland coastal plain from this threat, Gatlin asked Governor Clark to send an unspecified number of troops, as many as could be readily raised, to Goldsboro. On September 3, 1861, Governor Clark wired the War Department asking that it send two regiments, preferably North Carolina regiments, to New Bern and two more to Wilmington.[187] He followed with a letter explaining that General Gatlin had asked for as many more troops as could be spared but had not specified how many nor where to send them. Clark also observed that the North Carolina coast was too extensive for one commanding general, implying that North Carolina should be home to several command districts, each covering a strategic area of the coast.[188] Clark's requesting troops from the War Department was a somewhat unorthodox measure, considering that the state was primarily responsible for raising troops. Gatlin's request had been less than specific because Gatlin, not Clark, was responsible for deployment of troops. However, because Clark had no armed and ready regiments at his disposal, he apparently turned to the War Department for help, seemingly acting in Gatlin's stead. Earlier, Gatlin had remarked to Cooper that he had heard "indirectly," meaning from Governor Clark, that a regiment had been sent from Norfolk to Roanoke Island. It was becoming clear that the defense of eastern North Carolina required more closely coordinated communication among Clark, Gatlin and the War Department because coordination of efforts among the three was spotty this early in the war.

Before the War Department could consider Gatlin and Clark's requests, a false alarm diverted attention from their immediate needs. A rumor that Fort Macon was about to be abandoned had reached General Cooper, to which Cooper responded by ordering Gatlin to prevent such an abandonment at all costs. Where the rumor arose is unknown, possibly from some civilian correspondent, but Gatlin had just inspected Fort Macon on August 29, so he responded to General Cooper that the rumor was "devoid of all truth." He went on to describe to Cooper the immediate situation in eastern North Carolina. First, he explained to Cooper that although Fort Macon's men were raw recruits engaged in learning artillery skills, the fort could withstand a lengthy siege. Second, the enemy had strengthened its force on the sound side of Hatteras, making it difficult to "recover" the inlet. Third, because the Confederate navy had only two inferior boats at his disposal, he had arranged a private reconnaissance of Hatteras. Fourth, he was busily engaged in "fortifying the Neuse and Pamlico Rivers." Gatlin again urged the raising of a fleet of gunboats to patrol Pamlico Sound "without delay." He closed by advising Cooper that the fertile farmlands of Hyde and Tyrrell Counties would be pillaged unless protected by numerous troops and that running a telegraph line from Goldsboro to Morehead City was imperative.[189]

In response to Clark and Gatlin's earlier pleas, on September 3, 1861, the War Department commissioned Virginian Joseph Reid Anderson, an 1836 West Point graduate and the proprietor of the Tredegar Iron Works in Richmond, to brigadier general and assigned him to Gatlin's command. Anderson proceeded to Goldsboro with specific instructions to take charge of coast defenses of North Carolina.[190] His orders specified to hold reserve forces at Wilmington and Goldsboro, to erect a battery below New Bern and to outfit Roanoke Island with a battery to obstruct any entrance of the Union fleet into the Albemarle Sound. Gatlin intended to employ Anderson in continuing the coastal fortifications while he, Gatlin, concentrated on procuring men and arms and on administering the department. Gatlin still had not found time to set up his headquarters in Goldsboro, but as soon as Anderson arrived, he hoped to be able to do so.

Brigadier General Joseph Reid Anderson, Gatlin's subordinate general for the Cape Fear District. *Library of Congress.*

Then, on September 6, 1861, the Fort Macon alarm arose again. A British steamer off the coast reported that a Union fleet was on its way to attack Fort Macon. Gatlin immediately wired General Cooper of the news and departed the next day for New Bern. Cooper assured Gatlin that he had directed Governor Clark to send two newly raised regiments from Raleigh to Fort Macon. On September 8, 1861, Gatlin reported a small Yankee fleet anchored off Fort Macon and that he and General Anderson, who had arrived in New Bern, were going to Fort Macon the next morning. So far, no reinforcements had arrived from Raleigh. By the next morning, however, only a single Union ship lay off Fort Macon. Seeing that the whole incident had been another false alarm, Gatlin and Anderson returned from Fort Macon to Goldsboro. Gatlin notified General Cooper that a single rifled cannon, and no troops, had arrived at Fort Macon but that the emergency had ended.

In the midst of this latest Fort Macon threat, Governor Clark wrote to Secretary of War LeRoy P. Walker with two requests. The first was for the War Department to assign experienced artillery officers to the batteries at and around Wilmington. The second was to assign General D.H. Hill to command North Carolina's "Cape Fear forces," meaning the former Southern Coastal division with Wilmington at its core. Clark was not aware of General Anderson's exact duties, but he reiterated to Walker that the North Carolina coast was beyond the command scope of one general. By asking for D.H. Hill, Clark hoped to alleviate some of the pressure recently put on him from Wilmington correspondents, William S. Ashe among them, who begged him to do more to protect Wilmington. Wilmington's citizens apparently put the same type of pressure on the War Department as well, for on September 12, 1861, Secretary Walker wrote to Clark informing him that no regiments were available from Virginia for service in Wilmington and asking Clark instead to raise another new regiment for Wilmington service.

In subsequent correspondence to Adjutant General Samuel Cooper, Clark complained that General Gatlin, who on September 12, 1861, had just left from meeting with Clark in Raleigh, refused to send troops from his command into Hyde County to deal with growing Union sympathies in that region. Gatlin was still too preoccupied with the threat on Fort Macon to risk weakening his force in that area, but he wrote to Cooper on September 13 for advice on the matter. Cooper replied to Clark that as the general in charge, Gatlin should use his own discretion with regard to troop movements in his department.[191] Gatlin felt that the risk to Fort Macon outweighed the glaring Union sympathies in Hyde County and kept his force at Fort Macon intact. A mild but widening schism seemed to exist between Clark and Gatlin from that point forward, although Gatlin later did deploy several companies to Hyde County.

A lengthy newspaper column datelined "New Bern, N.C. September 9, 1861" and written by a reporter using the pen name of "Virginian" appeared in the *Charleston Mercury* on September 12. Apparently sent to cover the predicted attack on Fort Macon, the reporter turned instead to a synopsis of General Gatlin when the attack failed to materialize. In it, "Virginian" described Gatlin as *a military man, pure and simple, in the French sense of that term, that is, nothing else than a military man. All his ideas about men and things receive shape from his education. Everything is to be measured and governed by the rules and discipline of the camp. He has about as great a horror of the press as the monks had of Galileo…This sensitiveness in the General is pardonable, however, for I believe he is an excellent man, if he will only be skillful in defeating the Yankees, or in keeping them from invading and ravaging the coasts of North Carolina.*[192]

Gatlin certainly was a military man, but he was a military man from the old United States Army. He was used to getting troops and arms when needed. He was quickly learning that the Confederate army was not the old army.

With the Hatteras and Fort Macon crises at hand, Gatlin changed his personal plans for bringing his wife and children from Arkansas to Goldsboro. It would be October before Mary Ann would actually join Gatlin in Goldsboro, a delay from their original plan. Gatlin made time on September 4, 1861, to write from New Bern to Mary Ann in Fort Smith:

To Mrs. M.G. Gatlin
My Dear Little Wife,

I have had a very trying time for the last week. Have had scarcely time to bestow a thought upon you—that is saying a great deal. I had no sooner been placed in command of the Department of North Carolina than I was notified of an immense naval expedition having sailed south from Fortress Monroe, supposed for our coast. Sure enough it made its appearance off Fort Hatteras and after a bombardment of two days succeeded in reducing it. The garrison surrendered to the number of some 500. I arrived here but a few hours before the news of the surrender reached us. Although the distance to Hatteras is some 90 miles, the people were wild with excitement. Families were crowding the trains to get away from the enemy. Against all this panic I had little more to offer than a calm countenance but went to work at once to place this ancient city in a state of defense. Now confidence is restored and things are going on smoothly. I have, however, learned this much—that it is not probable that I shall be able to meet you at Memphis, so dear Mary you must get Bob [her brother] *a leave of absence and let him accompany you to Memphis. Recollect that it is to Goldsboro, N.C. that you are to telegraph me both from Little Rock and Memphis and when you arrive there to inquire my whereabouts.*

I would give a mint dear wife if you and the little ones were with me. I am so sorry that they and you have been sick. Kiss them a thousand times for me…

In haste, your affectionate husband,
R.C. Gatlin[193]

On September 13, 1861, General Gatlin was finally able to settle into his headquarters in Goldsboro. Gatlin's assistant adjutant general, Lieutenant Colonel Richard H. Riddick, was in Richmond delivering reports to the War Department, but Gatlin's aide-de-camp, First Lieutenant John Graham, son of former governor William Graham, joined Gatlin in Goldsboro. Gatlin rounded out his staff with Major John W. Cameron as his quartermaster and paymaster and Captain William W. Morrison as his subsistence officer. Gatlin's first duty was to report to the War Department an exact inventory and location of troops under his command. He reported to Richmond only 4,380 troops at his disposal, including 1,665 around Wilmington, 1,980 at Fort Macon, 605 at New Bern and 130 at Washington. In addition, General Huger had a regiment at Roanoke Island and a few men near Oregon Inlet. With his report, Gatlin asked for three more regiments to be placed at his disposal. The response from Richmond must have been negative, for on September 18, Gatlin advised Governor Clark that at least five new regiments were required from within North Carolina. With a frustrated air, he told Clark, "No reliance should be placed on the expectation of troops being sent back from Virginia, for I am told that none will be sent."[194] Little would change during the next six months, for the officials in Richmond were compelled to maintain troop strength around Norfolk and between Richmond and Washington, D.C., both of which were under constant threat of a Northern advance. In fairness to the Confederate War Department, Adjutant General Samuel Cooper seemed sympathetic to the needs of coastal North Carolina when, on September 5, 1861, he petitioned General Benjamin Huger, "Cannot you spare the sailors under your orders for duty on the coast of North Carolina?"[195] Huger responded in the negative, saying that he was already short-handed.

Aware of the vastness of his command, and realizing that the Confederacy would fill his ranks with only new in-state recruits rather than with experienced regiments, Gatlin turned to nagging Richmond for experienced officers. On September 18, 1861, he asked the War Department for two additional generals—one to take charge of the Cape Fear district and the other to command the coast from Bogue Banks northward to Roanoke Island. He intended to retain General Anderson as the engineer for the entire coast. William S. Ashe of Wilmington added his endorsement to Gatlin's request. In a letter to President Davis, Ashe asked for virtually the same thing, except that he suggested three rather than two coastal districts, with Anderson commanding one and James G. Martin and Colonel Gaston Meares, both North Carolinians, promoted to brigadier generals to command the other two—all under Gatlin's supervision. Jefferson Davis passed Ashe's proposal to the secretary of war, adding his recommendation for Gabriel J. Rains, another of Gatlin's old Seventh Infantry comrades and another North Carolinian, to be one of the commanding generals. The War Department acted on neither Gatlin's nor Ashe's request.

On September 20, 1861, yet another report of a Union armada headed for Fort Macon reached Gatlin. If another fleet were actually on the way, however, its destination could not be predicted with any certainty. Consequently, Gatlin ordered General Anderson to return to Wilmington and evidently decided to take direct command himself at Fort Macon or New Bern if either of those places came under attack. He quickly repeated his request to the War Department for two new generals to assist him. The Confederate commanders remained uncertain for several more days regarding the intentions of the Union attack force. Acting secretary of war Judah P. Benjamin exhorted Governor Clark to call out the militia from North Carolina's twelve northeastern counties and announced on September 23, 1861, that the War Department would assign General D.H. Hill to command the coast defenses of North Carolina. Back in Wilmington, General Anderson was so afraid that the fleet was destined to attack Wilmington's harbor that he wrote directly to General Cooper requesting that four regiments of infantry, three companies of cavalry and all the equipment to sustain them be sent immediately to Wilmington, plus two more regiments of infantry to be held at Goldsboro in reserve.[196] Had the threat materialized, the Federals in all likelihood could have chosen their destination and taken it, for no troops were forthcoming from Richmond. On September 24, 1861, Gatlin reported that six Union steamers lay off Fort Macon, but later that day, he was happy to report that all but two had disappeared. As quickly as it had arisen, the latest alarm of an attack on the North Carolina coast had ended.

Gatlin and Clark, rattled by the recurring false alarms, stepped up their demands on the War Department to do its duty, please, by North Carolina. Clark especially chastised the War Department for neglecting North Carolina.

He wrote to Judah Benjamin in the final week of September, stating that "if soldiers cannot be spared, I may at least hope that the requisitions for arms and powder and other munitions may be speedily and favorably attended to."[197] With rising ire, Clark reminded Benjamin of the many regiments and 13,500 stand of arms that North Carolina had sent to Virginia and warned Benjamin that "we are now out of arms, and our soil is invaded" and that "we have disarmed ourselves to arm you."[198] An obviously defensive Benjamin shot back at Clark for "the reproaches it has pleased you to lavish upon the executive department" by denying some of Clark's accusations and assuring him that the Confederate government had an "earnest desire" to defend North Carolina. Benjamin intimated, however, that Confederate resources were stretched very thin and suggested that Clark "aid in patriotic effort to defend your own coast by hearty co-operation."[199] One of Clark's chief complaints was that the Confederate navy was virtually nonexistent in North Carolina, to which Benjamin replied that not only did the navy ply the North Carolina sounds but also that new boats were being bought and outfitted specifically for North Carolina's defense. Apparently, Benjamin was more impressed with the strength of the emerging North Carolina naval squadron than were Clark and Gatlin. Still, Gatlin could claim significant improvements in the department during the month of September. The Union commander at Hatteras, Colonel Rush Hawkins, reported on September 17, 1861, that the Confederate Department of North Carolina was strengthening as follows:

> *1st. Since the taking of Hatteras, Fort Macon has been roofed with railroad iron, new guns added, and largely re-enforced. The town of Beaufort is now occupied by a large force; I believe that there are about 1,500 men at the fort and about 3,000 in and about the town. 2d. Fifteen vessels have been sunk in the Neuse River below New Berne. The fort or battery below the town of New Berne has been strengthened and new guns added; at the town there are two regiments of infantry, two or three squadrons of horse, and a section of artillery. 3d. Pamlico River has had a row of piles driven across it some 8 or 10 miles below the town of Washington; a small body of troops are stationed at this town. 4th. Roanoke Island has but one battery, instead of two, mounting seventeen guns, and a garrison of 2,200 men, and 800 more are expected there to-day from Norfolk.*[200]

At the Confederate War Department's insistence, Gatlin focused on Fort Macon. He had neither experienced officers nor extra troops at his disposal to send to Roanoke Island, so that crucial place lay fully exposed to the Yankee army at Hatteras. Thus, in early September 1861, General Huger in Norfolk, despite facing a mounting Union threat in his front, reluctantly allowed the Third Georgia Regiment, about 800 men under Colonel Ambrose R. Wright, to remain at Roanoke Island, which they had garrisoned at the time of the Hatteras loss. In addition, three raw companies of the Seventh North Carolina Volunteers were formed to serve, although not very comfortably, alongside the Third Georgians. Unknown to Gatlin until later, the 680-man Eighth North Carolina Regiment under Colonel Henry Shaw, on Governor Clark's orders, arrived at Roanoke Island on September 21, 1861. The only other Confederate force at Roanoke Island was a small navy. Confederate flag officer William F. Lynch of Virginia had replaced captured Commodore Samuel Barron on September 4, 1861. After journeying to New Bern to meet with Governor Clark and General Gatlin, Lynch hurried to Roanoke Island in mid-September to assume his command and begin arming Confederate gunboats. Lynch was keenly concerned with protecting Roanoke Island, for he knew holding it was the key to protecting the navy yard at Norfolk. Roanoke Island had received none of Gatlin's direct attention, so on September 26, 1861, Gatlin wrote to General Huger thanking him for filling the void and explaining that he had no regiments at present to replace the Third Georgia. Gatlin asked Huger to continue to improve the situation at Roanoke Island until his Department of North Carolina could assume responsibility.

In writing to Huger, Gatlin revealed also that he was not at all well. Recurring fever was a nemesis to him. He and T.H. Holmes had suffered from a malarial-like fever in the summer of 1834 while jointly supervising the construction of a military post in the Indian Territory. That fever placed both those young Seventh Infantry lieutenants on the "sick" roll at Fort Gibson. Then, in 1843, Gatlin suffered such a bad recurrence of that illness that he had been forced to take a ten-month furlough to the mountains of Virginia. He suffered other fever episodes during his army career, but they were of brief duration. On September 30, 1861, Gatlin wrote a letter to General Anderson in Wilmington, in which he complained, "I have exhausted my arguments with the authorities at Richmond for more troops." He concluded with an apology, stating that his letter "emanates from the brain of a sick man, scarcely able to be out of bed long enough to write it."[201]

On September 29, 1861, Adjutant General Cooper fulfilled Governor Clark's earlier request by issuing Special Order Number 166 assigning Brigadier General D.H. Hill to Gatlin's command and directing that Hill

General Daniel Harvey Hill, Gatlin's subordinate general for the Pamlico District. *Library of Congress.*

be "charged with the defense of that portion of the State lying between Albemarle Sound and the Neuse River and Pamlico Sound, including those waters."[202] Gatlin maintained his correspondence despite his illness, and as September wound down, he submitted an end-of-month report of his troop strength to the War Department. In it, he reported 5,272 troops under the command of General Anderson in the District of Cape Fear and 6,296 under the command of General D.H. Hill in the District of Pamlico. Based on subsequent reports, Gatlin's troop count seems exaggerated. Even if accurate, many of his department's regiments were untrained and poorly armed. Anderson, for example, from Wilmington, noted that his two newly received regiments were not ready for duty and that he had fewer than 600 men on each side of the Cape Fear River.

When General D.H. Hill arrived in Goldsboro, the recovering Gatlin was unsure if Hill's command included Roanoke Island, which drew its supplies more easily from Norfolk than from Raleigh or Goldsboro. Presuming that Huger would continue his temporary tenancy on Roanoke Island, but realizing the criticality of arming the back door to Norfolk, Gatlin urged the War Department to create a third North Carolina district, the Albemarle District, "embracing Roanoke Island and the Albemarle Sound," and to assign another experienced general to command it.[203] Gatlin had no choice but to neglect Roanoke Island, as long as he was intent on General Hill's strengthening the Pamlico Sound points of Fort Macon and New Bern. He was certain that General Huger was in a better position to manage Roanoke Island than he was. As his suggestion for an additional district languished in Richmond, the supervision of the entire coast from the Virginia border to the Neuse River fell to Hill. Undaunted, Hill endorsed a renewed plea by Gatlin to greatly increase the "armament of Fort Macon"[204] and then, beginning on October 2, 1861, embarked on a lengthy inspection tour of his vast command at Fort Macon. As had Gatlin and Clark before him, Hill requisitioned the War Department for big guns, trained artillerists and additional troops for Fort Macon. When he received no reply, Hill directed his requisition request to Governor Clark. State Adjutant General James G. Martin replied for Clark that Hill should unquestionably requisition the Confederate government for arms and ammunition because the state had none to give.

While Gatlin, Clark and the War Department busied themselves with threats against Fort Macon in September, the Union army strengthened its position at Hatteras Inlet and outfitted boats for use on North Carolina's sounds. Federal navy secretary Gideon Welles announced on October 3, 1861, that the tug *Underwriter*, commanded by Lieutenant R.B. Lowry, was on its way to Hampton Roads as one of the boats to be used for "the inside waters of North Carolina."[205] Ensconced on the Outer Banks, flamboyant Colonel Rush Hawkins of the Ninth New York Zouaves commanded upward of one thousand troops with an eye to ousting the Confederates from their refuge on Roanoke Island.[206] On September 20, 1861, Hawkins received warning of a Confederate plan to retake Hatteras. As a deterrent against any Confederate advance from Roanoke Island, he ordered the Twentieth Indiana Regiment to encamp at the village of Chicamacomico, just south of Oregon Inlet between Roanoke Island and Hatteras Inlet. The Confederates were considering just such an advance, although it is not clear who was fully responsible for promoting it. Colonel Ambrose R. Wright of the Third Georgia

Volunteers commanded the troops on Roanoke Island, and Commodore William Lynch joined him with a small fleet of converted tugboats. Perhaps during his early September discussions with General Gatlin and Governor Clark, Lynch had received tacit approval from them to launch an amphibious effort to retake Hatteras. More likely, Wright and Lynch concocted the plan themselves. At any rate, Wright and Lynch combined forces to engage the Federals with Third Georgians crewing Lynch's three boats: the *Raleigh*, the *Curlew* and the *Junaluska*.

On October 1, 1861, Lynch's little fleet outlasted and captured the Union supply boat *Fanny* in a brief naval encounter just off Oregon Inlet, within sight of the camp at Chicamacomico. Lynch and Wright's next move would be to surround the Yankees of the Twentieth Indiana Regiment at Chicamacomico by landing Third Georgians north of the camp and Eighth North Carolinians south of the camp. On October 4, 1861, the Georgians and a company of Seventh North Carolina Volunteers hit the sound-side beach north of Chicamacomico and drove the startled and outmanned Yankees southward into the waiting guns of the Eighth North Carolina. However, the Eighth North Carolina had not yet appeared; its men were stuck on shoals south of Chicamacomico, too far from shore to make a landing. Disconcerted by the absence of the Eighth North Carolina, the Georgians camped for the night and began a retreat the next morning, only to be surprised themselves by the appearance of Yankees in their rear. A much-reinforced Yankee army rushed northward on the heels of the Confederates, who had to outrace the combined Twentieth Indiana and Ninth New York regiments and dodge heavy fire from Union ships now just offshore. Colonel Wright's Confederates made it to waiting boats, and most escaped back to Roanoke Island. This ended the Confederate effort to recapture Hatteras Inlet. The aborted affair earned the nickname the "Chicamacomico Races," much to the embarrassment of the Confederacy.

Wright and Lynch did not abandon their fervor for recapturing Hatteras Inlet and consulted with General Huger about it. However, General D.H. Hill, now responsible for Roanoke Island, squelched a second attempt by Wright and Lynch with an order on October 17, 1861, stating that "no expedition for offensive operations will be undertaken without my sanction and authority."[207] Public sentiment demanded a recapture of Hatteras, and Governor Clark cautiously endorsed it as well. Captain Josiah S. Pender of the Tenth North Carolina Artillery presented a plan for recapturing Hatteras to Adjutant General James G. Martin, who asked General Gatlin his opinion of it. Gatlin had not seen the plan and thus would not comment on it.

Major General Benjamin Huger, commander of the Confederacy's Norfolk Department, including Roanoke Island and several northeastern North Carolina counties. *Library of Congress.*

Gatlin and Hill took a more defensive stance. Holding a recaptured Hatteras with too few troops, ineffective cannon and a weak navy, especially after the Chicamacomico fiasco, seemed inconceivable to them. Running the Yankees off the Outer Banks consumed much talk, but no further attempt was made to do so. Hill continued his inspection tour in Hyde County and Roanoke Island and then went to Portsmouth, Virginia, to solicit help from General Huger and navy secretary Mallory in procuring heavy artillery. From Portsmouth, he reiterated the criticality of holding Roanoke Island and declared his "entire inability…to hold the line intrusted [*sic*] to my care."[208]

On October 21, 1861, a telegram from General Cooper, via General Huger, warned that a Union fleet was en route from New York to attack

Beaufort and New Bern. Gatlin alerted Hill in New Bern and Anderson in Wilmington, and the three of them scrambled for the next four days trying to guess the point or points of attack and to find men and guns enough to defend those points. Gatlin wrote to Hill on October 25, 1861, "I have made so many requisitions on the Ordnance Department at Richmond for guns and powder without obtaining anything that I am not disposed to do so again."[209] Hill completed the inspection of his district with a visit to Swansboro on October 28, 1861, and made a full report to Gatlin. He urged Gatlin to send a regiment to occupy the Outer Banks above Hatteras and again raised his concerns about Roanoke Island, insisting that two North Carolina regiments must replace the existing defenders because General Huger was anxious to recall his Third Georgians to Suffolk. Gatlin had to apologize to Hill, stating that no more regiments were available from North Carolina and that two regiments promised from Virginia came with distinct orders to remain in reserve at Goldsboro. It had taken Hill virtually the entire month of October to travel the length of his district. Clearly, a district that included the critical points of New Bern and Roanoke Island and that took weeks to traverse was too large for one general to manage.

On October 28, 1861, word came that Wilmington was to be the Yankee target. General Anderson in Wilmington quickly fired off a demand to the War Department for large amounts of ammunition and an experienced artillerist, noting that the War Department had not yet filled his ordnance requisition from the previous month. Secretary of War Benjamin sent ammunition to Anderson by special train the following day. While Anderson was preparing to repulse an attack at Wilmington, Gatlin and Hill were cautiously alert to a possible strike at Fort Macon instead. Hill asked Gatlin to meet with him and Commodore Lynch in New Bern to discuss launching an amphibious assault to recapture Hatteras. However, Gatlin had charge of reserve troops in Goldsboro, and with the destination of the Federal fleet still in question, he felt compelled to remain at his headquarters until the attack point was more certain. He relied on Hill to act for him in any decision made with Lynch. As October waned, the officers of the Department of North Carolina were agitated at the Confederacy's now-obvious failure or inability to meet the needs of North Carolina's defense.

November 1861 opened with Governor Clark again lambasting Secretary of War Benjamin for the Confederacy's neglectful treatment of North Carolina. At Gatlin's request, Clark was obligingly raising six new regiments and four artillery companies to repel the impending invasion of his state, but the regiments would not be ready for service until armed.

Brigadier General James Green Martin, the adjutant general who raised most of North Carolina's regiments in 1861–62. *Library of Congress.*

Simultaneously, the First North Carolina Regiment's enlistment was nearing completion. Clark perceived that Benjamin not only was not going to provide arms for the new regiments but also was going to commandeer the guns of the retiring North Carolina regiment. Clark was furious that North Carolina had sent so many men and arms to Virginia and now would receive none back. He accused the Confederacy of arming Virginia at North Carolina's expense. When Benjamin replied in a conciliatory tone, Clark calmed down, but the rancor between North Carolina's statehouse and the Confederate government would continue through the next governor's administration and on to the end of the war.

Sniping also arose between North Carolina adjutant general James G. Martin and General Hill. In response to the approaching Union fleet, Hill called out the militia from several coastal plain counties and had them muster in New Bern. However, Martin took exception to Hill's action and wrote to Gatlin asking Gatlin to release the militia units, which both Martin and Gatlin considered unready. Gatlin met with Hill in New Bern on November 5 and 6 and, while defending Hill's action to Martin as quite reasonable given the impending attack, directed Hill to release the units. Hill later posted a letter in the *North Carolina Standard* defending his decision.[210] Hill, it seems, was growing frustrated with the situation in North Carolina. The Confederate War Department virtually ignored Gatlin and Hill, both of whom received a goodly share of second-guessing from the governor's office. Hill increasingly disdained the indolence shown by so many coastal North Carolinians and their complacency toward the Confederate cause. He was losing patience with his role in North Carolina.

Of primary concern, however, was the destination of the Union fleet. One of the fleet's ships ran aground on November 2, 1861, off Fort Macon. Interrogation of the ship's captured crew revealed that the Union aimed its attack not at North Carolina but at Port Royal, South Carolina. On November 4, 1861, before departing for New Bern to meet with General Hill, Gatlin alerted the governor and the War Department of this new information. The War Department immediately ordered General Anderson in Wilmington to send two of his regiments, Clingman's and Radcliff's, and Moore's artillery battery to South Carolina. It also immediately recalled Gatlin's two reserve regiments from Goldsboro back to Richmond. The Union fleet attacked and captured Port Royal on November 7, 1861.

During November 1861, some notable changes took place. In the North, General George McClellan assumed command of the Union army on November 1, 1861. In the South, Robert E. Lee became commander of the South Carolina, Georgia and Northern Florida Coastal Department on November 5. Perhaps more significantly for eastern North Carolina, the Confederate command recalled General D.H. Hill to Virginia on November 16. In less than two months, Hill had done much to shore up the defenses of North Carolina's coast. Ironically, his pet project had been to make Roanoke Island impregnable, but before he could fulfill that desire, he was gone. In Hill's place, the Confederacy promoted and appointed Colonel Lawrence O'Bryan Branch. Branch was the nephew of a former North Carolina governor and had been a lawyer in Florida and a North Carolina legislator. He was North Carolina's quartermaster general from

Brigadier General Lawrence O'Bryan Branch, who replaced D.H. Hill as Gatlin's subordinate general for the Pamlico Department. Branch commanded Gatlin's Confederate army in the Battle of New Bern in March 1862 and was later killed at Antietam. *Library of Congress.*

May 1861 to September 1861, when he assumed command of the Thirty-third North Carolina Regiment. His political familiarity to the Confederate hierarchy probably landed him the open brigadier generalship. Though extremely intelligent and energetic, Branch had little military experience. Lieutenant Colonel Henry Burgwyn of the Twenty-sixth North Carolina described Branch as "not competent."[211]

Unfortunately, especially for him and Gatlin, on November 26, 1861, the War Department ordered Branch to relieve General Huger of the de facto responsibility Huger had held at Roanoke Island since the beginning of the war. Huger was authorized to recall the Third Georgia Regiment from Roanoke Island to Norfolk. Gatlin arranged to transfer the few companies of the Seventeenth North Carolina Regiment (formerly the Seventh North Carolina Volunteers) then in Hyde County to Roanoke Island and assigned the newly formed Thirty-first North Carolina Regiment, Colonel John V. Jordan's regiment, from Beaufort County to replace the departing Georgians. Again raising an old request, Gatlin implored the War Department, in a letter dated November 29, 1861, to create a third district from the Neuse River south to the New River and that Colonel Reuben P. Campbell, commander of the Seventh North Carolina Regiment, be promoted to brigadier general to assume command of the new district.[212] Independently, on that same day, a group of concerned citizens from Washington, North Carolina, petitioned the War Department for a new northeastern department.

While things in North Carolina were in organizational flux, Union general McClellan and his old friend General Ambrose E. Burnside were cooking up a scheme to invade eastern North Carolina and neutralize the important Wilmington & Weldon Railroad, which supplied the Confederacy with troops and supplies from North Carolina.

The recall of Huger's Third Georgia Regiment put a terrific strain on the already overextended and undermanned Gatlin. General Anderson in Wilmington pressed for replacements for the regiments he had sent to South Carolina, but Gatlin had no one to send him. Colonel Jordan had the not fully organized Thirty-first North Carolina Regiment in Beaufort County. Only partially armed, it proceeded to Roanoke Island on December 12, 1861, just in time to see the Third Georgia depart. Gatlin needed three more batteries—one for Huggins Island, one for the Neuse River and one for the Pamlico River—but Governor Clark could send no one. Gatlin went to Wilmington in mid-month to confer with Anderson. In the meantime, Clark wrote twice to Gatlin expressing concern over the status of Roanoke Island. Colonel Henry Shaw, commanding the Eighth North Carolina Regiment on Roanoke Island, felt exposed and wrote so to Gatlin. Returning from Wilmington on December 20, 1861, Gatlin addressed both Clark and Shaw. He wrote to Governor Clark:

> *It is to be regretted that General Hill should have been removed just as he was about placing that post in a proper state of defense...The necessary orders will be given at once to place Roanoke Island in a proper state for defense, and an engineer sent to superintend the works. I have given orders for the blocking up of a part of Croatan Sound, and I presume the work is now going on.*[213]

In that letter, Gatlin reiterated that Jordan's Thirty-first North Carolina Regiment continued to be only partially armed and that guns, powder and percussion caps were needed at once, possibly from North Carolina troops whose service had ended. Roanoke Island was becoming an exasperating problem for Gatlin.

Then, on December 21, 1861, the Roanoke Island situation took a major turn when the War Department announced a departmental reorganization:

> *SPECIAL ORDERS ADJT. AND INSPR GENERALS OFFICE,*
> *No. 272.*
> *Richmond, Va., December 21, 1861.*
>
> * * * * * * *
>
> *8. That part of North Carolina east of the Chowan River, together with the counties of Washington and Tyrrell, is hereby constituted a military district, under Brigadier-General Wise, and attached to the command of Major-General Huger, commanding the Department of Norfolk.*
> *9. That part of the coast of North Carolina between the above-described district and Bogue Inlet will form a separate military district, under Brigadier-General Branch, and the remainder of the coast of North Carolina a district under Brig. Gen. Joseph H. Anderson. These two last districts will remain, as heretofore, attached to the command of Brigadier-General Gatlin.*
> * * * * * * *
>
> *By command of the Secretary of War:*
> *JNO. WITHERS, Assistant Adjutant- General.*[211]

Confederate officials had finally heeded Gatlin's advice, thanks in large part to a December 9, 1861 endorsement by North Carolina judge Asa Biggs, and formed a third district in North Carolina, the Division of the Albemarle, composed of the northeastern counties of Chowan, Perquimans, Pasquotank, Gates, Camden, Currituck, Washington and Tyrrell. Roanoke Island was then in Currituck County. Gatlin did not command the Albemarle Division, however. Defense of that part of the state now fell to the Department of Norfolk under General Benjamin Huger, with Virginia's ex-governor Brigadier General Henry Wise commanding. Wise was one of a number of political generals appointed by President Davis who had little or no military experience. Still, he had raised a regiment known as Wise's

Legion and had performed well in western Virginia earlier in the war. Wise was astute enough to recognize that Roanoke Island was the key to both eastern North Carolina, with its rich agricultural resources, and Norfolk, with its critical shipyards, but he would not be able to inspect the island until after the first of the year. Until Wise could take command formally and visit Roanoke Island, Gatlin and Clark continued to supervise the activities of Colonels Shaw and Jordan in preparing the island for probable invasion.

Brigadier General Henry A. Wise of Virginia commanded the Albemarle District of the Department of Norfolk under General Huger. *Library of Congress.*

By the end of December, the sparse Confederate army in North Carolina was widely dispersed. In addition to the two regiments and three companies at Roanoke Island, Colonel Reuben Campbell's Seventh and Colonel Zebulon Vance's Twenty-sixth Regiments were at Bogue Banks with five artillery companies under Colonel Moses White and three companies of the Twenty-seventh North Carolina at nearby Fort Macon. Seven more regiments of the Twenty-seventh and eight companies of the Second North Carolina Cavalry were at New Bern, and the Twenty-fourth Georgia Regiment was at Washington, North Carolina, along with two companies of the Second North Carolina Cavalry and four artillery companies stationed along the Pamlico. In Wilmington, General Anderson had three North Carolina infantry regiments—the Twentieth, Twenty-eighth and Thirtieth—plus a cavalry unit and artillery units at the various forts and batteries. Thus, of thirty-seven regiments raised in North Carolina, only nine remained in the state. Gatlin had fewer than eight thousand troops in his command.

Meanwhile, at the Union's Fortress Monroe near Norfolk, practically in Huger's backyard, General Burnside was finalizing his preparations for an amphibious attack on North Carolina. Rumors began to reach Gatlin that the "Burnside Expedition" was on the way. The weather turned chilly, and Christmas came and went without military activity to break its peaceful spell. However, the war in eastern North Carolina would heat up again before the temperatures would.

Chapter 13

"North Carolina Has to Fight Her Own Battles": The Burnside Expedition

January became a month of nervous guessing, preparation and waiting in North Carolina. Word had reached Gatlin and Clark that the Federals, under Burnside, were preparing to launch an assault on the North Carolina coast. The exact point of attack was not certain, but it would be one or more of Fort Macon, New Bern, Roanoke Island or Wilmington. Gatlin's calculated guess was that New Bern was in no danger until after the Union had neutralized Roanoke Island. Roanoke Island was now out of Gatlin's jurisdiction, so his immediate concern was New Bern. In a January 3, 1862 letter to Governor Clark, he requested that Clark send the newly formed regiments at Raleigh, the Thirty-third and Thirty-fifth Regiments under Clark Avery and James Sinclair, to General Branch at New Bern. He also asked Clark to send the Thirty-fourth Regiment under Colonel Collett Leventhorpe to General Anderson at Wilmington. Gatlin further urged, "The force at New Berne ought to be immediately increased in consequence of the reported preparations to invade that section of the State. It is sad to think of our deficiency of troops to repel invasion."[215]

That same day, January 3, 1862, General Henry Wise embarked on his first trip to Roanoke Island. He wrote to Secretary Benjamin in Richmond asking for additional pile drivers "to obstruct the Roanoke and Croatan Sounds" and to complain that General Huger's troops around Norfolk expended enough powder in target practice to supply the entire needs of Roanoke Island.[216]

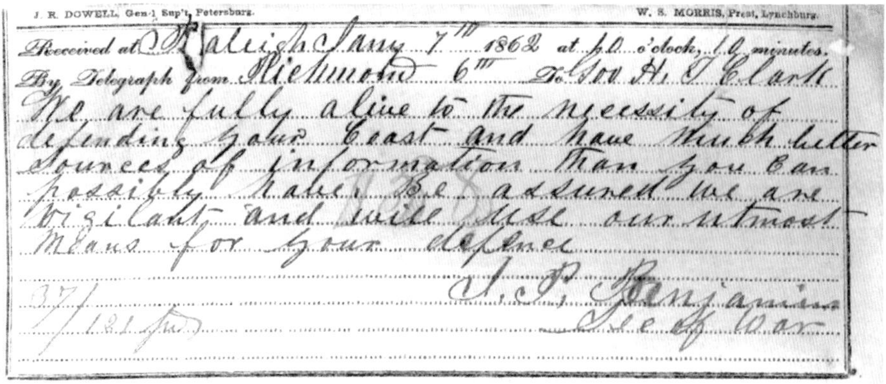

J. R. DOWELL, Gen'l Sup't, Petersburg. W. S. MORRIS, Prest, Lynchburg.

Received at Raleigh Jany 7th 1862 at 10 o'clock, 10 minutes.
By Telegraph from Richmond 6th To Gov H. T. Clark
We are fully alive to the necessity of defending your Coast and have much better sources of information than you can possibly have. Be assured we are vigilant and will use our utmost means for your defence
J. P. Benjamin
Sec of War
37/121 pd

A January 17, 1862 telegram from Confederate secretary of war Judah Benjamin to North Carolina governor Henry Clark promising Confederate help for North Carolina. Little help arrived. *North Carolina Archives.*

A cautious Gatlin advised General Branch in New Bern on January 10, 1862, to be on the alert and to report any enemy sightings so that Gatlin could send reinforcements. Gatlin had to juggle his regiments carefully because he had so few and the points of potential attack were so many. He did order Company A of the Third North Carolina Artillery, the Lenoir Braves, directly to New Bern to operate one of the batteries.[217] In another letter to Branch, dated January 13, 1862, Gatlin approved Branch's suggestions for strengthening the defenses of New Bern. He also pleaded with Branch to step up surveillance efforts in the outlying areas where Union troops might land.[218] With one eye cautiously open to a possible attack on Wilmington, Gatlin stayed in touch with General Anderson. He advised Anderson in a January 14, 1862 dispatch that he was retaining the Thirty-fourth North Carolina in Goldsboro as a reserve force. Gatlin still exhibited a glimmer of faith in the Confederate War Department when he requested from Anderson, "Give me immediate notice should the enemy appear, and I will draw troops from New Berne and demand re-enforcements from Richmond."[219]

In response to the emergency, Gatlin ordered Colonel Leventhorpe to march his Thirty-fourth North Carolina Regiment and several other new regiments from Raleigh to Wilmington and to New Bern. Leventhorpe stopped in Goldsboro as ordered and, upon meeting Gatlin for the first time, was impressed with his commanding general. Leventhorpe wrote, "Goldsboro, Jan. 15th '62. General Gatlin called on me today. He is a very nice gentleman, about 51 or 52. He looks like a real soldier."[220]

The Department of North Carolina was plagued constantly by unfilled requisitions and late deliveries from the Confederate War Department. On January 15, 1862, when muskets promised for two regiments of volunteers had not yet reached Goldsboro, Gatlin complained to Governor Clark, "These repeated delays and failures to fill requisitions must prove fatal to us."[221] Then, the Burnside Expedition made its appearance. On January 17, 1862, Gatlin wired the following to Confederate adjutant general Samuel Cooper: "General Branch reports that he has received information of forty-two steamers and three sail vessels lying at Hatteras. Many of them arrived last Saturday."[222] Although he was fairly certain that New Bern, and not Wilmington, would be a target of the Burnside Expedition, Gatlin held two regiments in reserve at Goldsboro—the Thirty-fourth North Carolina and the Thirty-seventh North Carolina—to reinforce by train either New Bern or Wilmington, whichever was attacked first. However, both reserve regiments were poorly armed, wracked with measles and mumps and not yet combat ready. An anxious Gatlin expressed his army's predicament concisely on January 18, 1862, in missives to Governor Clark and General Anderson:

> [To Clark] *It looks very much like a determination to attack the whole of our Sound coast. Of course, I will go down whenever the enemy show where they intend to attack. I am much concerned about the arms of the Thirty-fourth and Thirty-seventh Regiments. I have telegraphed twice on the subject. A reply dated yesterday says the subject will be brought to the notice of the Secretary of War.*[223]

> [To Anderson] *Before attempting New Berne…I am clearly of opinion that they must reduce Roanoke Island…More than ten days ago I wrote to the Adjutant-General, drawing his attention to the condition of our defenses, and begging that a reserve force be sent here to be sent to the point attacked. To this I have received no reply. It is very discouraging, and I see plainly that North Carolina has to fight her own battles notwithstanding the large force she has sent to Virginia, South Carolina, and Tennessee. If we are invaded, there is nothing for it but that we turn out to a man and drive off the invader.*[224]

For the next several days, reports of varying numbers of Federal ships arriving and anchoring off Hatteras Inlet trickled in to General Branch. As few as twenty-four steamers were reported and as many as seventy-seven. After conferring with Branch, Gatlin feared that the size of the

Major General Ambrose E. Burnside, Union commander of the expedition that conquered and occupied eastern North Carolina. *Library of Congress.*

Burnside armada was much larger than anticipated.[225] On January 20, 1862, Gatlin fired off two letters to Adjutant General Cooper in Richmond. In the first, he complained that General Branch had no boat with which to spy on the Union position, that the Confederate navy had no presence on the North Carolina sounds, that arms for his two reserve regiments had not arrived and that a large columbiad cannon destined for Fort Macon had been delayed by negligent railroad agents. In the second, he reported that three Outer Banks boat pilots who had escaped from Union impressment warned him that the Burnside Expedition was targeting "New Bern, Washington, Hyde County, and Roanoke" and that the expedition was already underway.[226]

Once Gatlin was certain, on January 20, 1862, that Burnside had launched his forces from Hatteras Inlet, he wrote to General Branch at New Bern:

> *The Burnside expedition has at length made its appearance in our waters. I have forwarded the information by telegraph to Richmond, Raleigh, and Norfolk. Asked for arms and re-enforcements. I will be with you should they come on the Neuse. Keep Campbell's and Vance's regiments ready to move up should they be required*[227]*...I would come down to-night, but I hardly think they would dare to leave Roanoke Island in their rear; so in my opinion you can proceed with deliberation, though zealously, in your defenses. I am fearful that our northeastern counties are lost. It is sad to think how obstinate the authorities at Richmond have been in regard to the destination of the fleet.*[228]

Gatlin knew that to prevent a naval counterattack, Burnside would have to dislodge the Confederates from Roanoke Island before attempting other points. However, Roanoke Island had not been Gatlin's responsibility since December 21, 1861. He had all he could do to concentrate on strengthening his New Bern batteries. The Department of Norfolk generals, Huger and Wise, would have to plead with Richmond for help. Gatlin, convinced that Roanoke Island was lost, began moving his forces into position to defend New Bern. He already had Colonel Reuben Campbell's Seventh North Carolina and Colonel Zebulon Vance's Twenty-sixth North Carolina Regiments encamped at Bogue Banks near Beaufort, and he sent the new, unarmed Thirty-seventh North Carolina under Colonel Charles C. Lee to General Branch at New Bern. Gatlin urged Branch to call out the militia from several surrounding counties and muster them at Washington.

On January 22, 1862, the arms Gatlin had requested for the Thirty-fourth and Thirty-seventh Regiments arrived in Goldsboro, but six hundred of the one thousand muskets were of the old-fashioned flint-and-steel variety, not fitted with newer and more effective percussion caps. The Thirty-seventh had already moved on down to New Bern, and Burnside was on the Albemarle Sound, so Gatlin had no time to send the guns back to Fayetteville for refitting. Gatlin also let Branch know that his health was "much improved." Apparently, Gatlin had been ill again.[229]

On January 24, 1862, Gatlin sent a status report to Governor Clark. In it, he accused the War Department of indifference to North Carolina's peril. He bemoaned, "I have more than once asked for re-enforcements without eliciting a reply of any kind. Consequently, I infer that we are to be left to fight our own battles. Hence, we must raise as many troops as we can arm."[230]

For several days, the Burnside fleet continued to gather at Hatteras Inlet until by January 24, 1862, 175 vessels of all sorts had assembled. Fortunately for the Confederates, one of the most violent nor'easters in decades erupted off the Outer Banks, thrashing and dashing Burnside's armada and delaying any attack he had planned. Hoping to take advantage of Burnside's misfortune, Gatlin begged Richmond one more time:

> *I have the honor to report that a storm of great violence has been prevailing upon our coast since early on the night of the 22nd instant; it has doubtless damaged the enemy at Hatteras, and it may be will derange his plans for some days. As there can be no doubt but that the Burnside expedition is intended to operate in our sounds, it becomes a matter of vital importance to us to consider the means in our power to resist his advance upon the main-lands, and if the force now in the State is insufficient, to try to provide for the deficiency and that speedily...Satisfied that the expedition is of such a magnitude that to resist it successfully we ought to have a large increase to our present force, I am constrained to renew my application of the 3rd instant, viz, that a large reserve, with an experienced commander, be at once sent to this point and placed at my disposal. Hoping that the War Department will take speedy action in the matter, I remain, sir, very respectfully, your obedient servant…*[231]

Unfortunately, the storm that had battered Burnside also further delayed the much-overdue defensive preparations on Roanoke Island—not that General Huger was very active in that endeavor, anyway. When he received three new batteries of artillery from the War Department, Huger refused to furnish water transportation for them to Roanoke Island. He insisted that the guns be hauled overland. Aside from sending those batteries in the slowest manner possible, Huger left the entire defense of Roanoke Island to General Henry Wise. Wise first visited Roanoke Island on January 7. Realizing immediately the weakness of the place, he petitioned General Huger for cannon and 4,500 more troops. Between the Eighth and Thirty-first North Carolina Regiments and his own Wise's Legion, Wise at that time had only 1,500 men under his command. A nervous Huger refused to release to Wise any of the 15,000 idle, unassigned and armed troops in garrison at Suffolk, less than one hundred miles away.[232]

By month's end, Gatlin fully expected that if Roanoke Island were to fall, the rivers of the Albemarle Sound would be open to Yankee ascension. He desperately hoped to prevent Burnside from steaming up the Roanoke River and destroying the railroad bridge at Weldon. To Adjutant General Cooper, on January 30, 1862, Gatlin advised placing batteries at key locations along the Roanoke River below Weldon, at least as far downriver as Halifax to stop any Yankee attempt on Weldon. Gatlin, however, could do no more than send an engineer to the river. He had at his disposal no troops or batteries not already critically deployed elsewhere.[233]

At January's close, Gatlin's total command included 3,565 men present for duty at twelve locations in the Cape Fear District under General Anderson, 7,516 men at eight locations in the Pamlico District under General Branch and 792 men of the Thirty-fourth North Carolina in reserve at Goldsboro for a total of 11,873 effective but poorly armed troops.[234]

February 1862 opened with a vain plea from Governor Clark to Secretary Benjamin for two or three regiments from the Virginia peninsula to help repel the coming Burnside assault on Roanoke Island. Clark also derided Benjamin for the Confederacy's negligence in preparing Roanoke Island's defenses, implying that neither Gatlin nor Wise was an efficient officer.[235] Benjamin, of course, replied that the War Department was doing everything within its power to defend eastern North Carolina, finally admitting that the Confederacy was short on munitions and ordnance and was woefully outmanned. He did promise, however, to send up to three thousand men from Huger's command to Wise at Roanoke Island and to send a regiment from Petersburg to Gatlin in Goldsboro.[236]

The Confederacy's inattention to the Burnside Expedition did prove fatal to eastern North Carolina and ultimately to the South as well. In early February, the Richmond newspapers reported that the storm had destroyed Burnside's fleet and that providence had intervened on the South's behalf. However, on February 5, 1862, seemingly from the edge of oblivion, Burnside approached little Roanoke Island with sixty-seven ships and 13,000 infantry troops. Confederate commodore William F. Lynch waited just off the island with his eight-boat makeshift fleet, and Wise had only 1,473 men on the island. Wise was ill and confined to bed across the Albemarle Sound on Nags Head, where he held another 1,500 troops, reinforcements from the Second North Carolina and from two Virginia regiments that had arrived in late January.[237]

Rain and cold on February 5, 1862, temporarily insulated the men of the Second North Carolina, Eighth North Carolina, Thirty-first North Carolina, elements of the Seventeenth North Carolina and two Virginia regiments on Roanoke Island from the Burnside Expedition. Fog delayed Burnside's approach the next day, too, but on the morning of February 7, the fog broke. Burnside closed in and engaged the Confederate land battery and Lynch's eight-boat navy in an all-day artillery duel. That evening, after the ferocious artillery fire had ceased, the Yankees landed on the

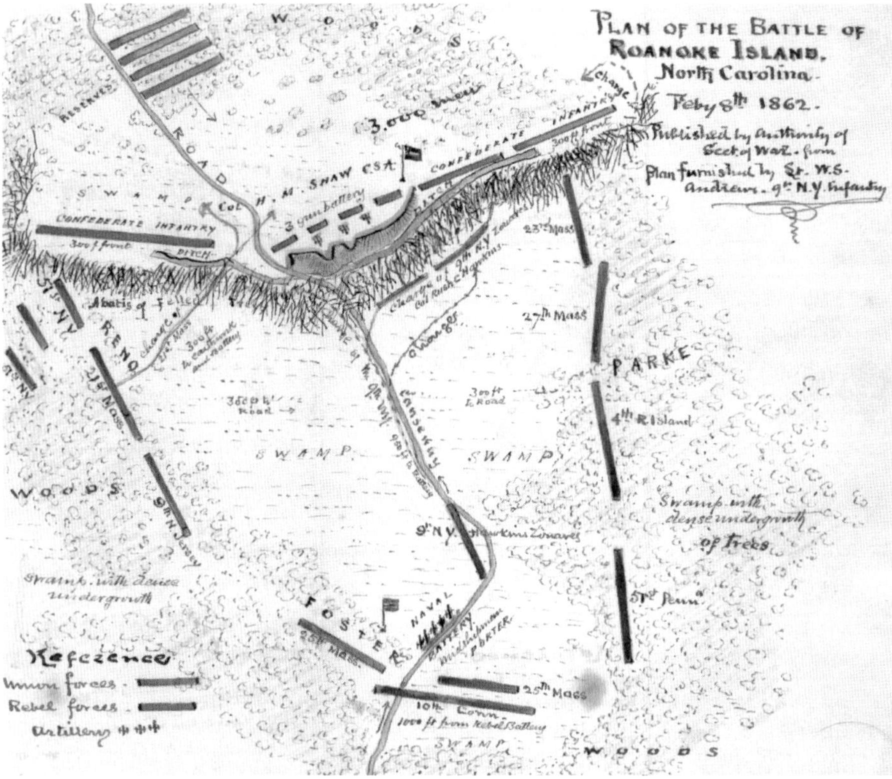

Above: Union map plan for the Battle of Roanoke Island. *Library of Congress*.

Left: Colonel Henry M. Shaw of the Eighth North Carolina Regiment commanded Confederate troops in the Battle of Roanoke Island. He was captured, paroled and later killed in action. *Library of Congress*.

The Burnside Expedition landing at Roanoke Island, February 7, 1862, as sketched by A.J. Richards, Company K, Eighth Regiment Connecticut Volunteers. *Library of Congress.*

southwest side of Roanoke Island and went ashore in three brigades led by Generals John G. Foster, Jesse L. Reno and John G. Parke. The following day, February 8, Confederate colonel Henry M. Shaw, commanding in Wise's absence, held out admirably for as long as he could, but when Reno's brigade waded through a supposedly impassable swamp and flanked Shaw's right wing, the day was lost. Shaw surrendered the island. Burnside lost 37 killed and 214 wounded, while Shaw lost 24 killed, 68 wounded and 2,500 men taken prisoner, including 600 reinforcements who had shown up just in time to be captured.[238]

Still unwell, Wise, with his remaining three companies and an uncounted number of Confederate soldiers who had escaped the battle site, scrambled up the Outer Banks to Virginia.[239] A Confederate board of inquiry later exonerated Wise for the loss of Roanoke Island and laid the blame at the feet of Secretary of War Judah P. Benjamin and General Huger, noting that they had received timely and adequate warning but had failed to prepare an adequate defense. General Wise, disgusted with General Huger's inattention to the newly formed Albemarle District, went over Huger's head to Richmond to testify regarding the loss of Roanoke Island. Wise told the War Department that he accused General Huger of doing "nothing, nothing, nothing."[240] Wise felt strongly that Roanoke Island was of such strategic importance to the South that "it should have been defended at the expense of 20,000 men and of many millions of dollars."[241]

Commodore Lynch, out of ammunition and hoping to reach Norfolk to refit his fleet, tried to salvage his six remaining boats by sailing up the Pasquotank River toward the Dismal Swamp Canal. Union commander Stephen Rowan closely followed Lynch, and on February 10, 1862, Rowan and Lynch clashed at Elizabeth City. It was no contest. Rowan destroyed four of Lynch's boats and then occupied Elizabeth City. The CSS *Appomattox* escaped and tried to make it to Norfolk but could not fit through the Dismal Swamp Canal locks. Only the CSS *Beaufort* made it back to Norfolk. The so-called Mosquito Fleet was no more. From that day on, the waters of North Carolina belonged to the Yankees. Two days later, on February 12, 1862, the Yankees occupied Edenton, and then on February 19, Colonel Rush Hawkins and his Ninth New York Zouaves marched into and burned the town of Winton.[242] For the next four weeks, Burnside prepared for the crowning blow of his expedition: New Bern.

Following the loss of Roanoke Island, Generals Gatlin and Branch knew all too well what to expect next, but Jeff Davis was too concerned with Confederate losses in Tennessee and the threat of McClellan in the Virginia Peninsula to pay much heed to North Carolina. The War Department did order the Twenty-fourth North Carolina Regiment from Petersburg to Weldon to protect the vital bridge and rail line, but it failed to notify Gatlin. In the meantime, now that the Roanoke River was accessible to Burnside from the Albemarle Sound, Gatlin ordered Colonel Leventhorpe's Thirty-fourth North Carolina from Goldsboro to Halifax to block the river, and he ordered the newly formed Thirty-eighth North Carolina, under Colonel William J. Hoke, to Weldon. On February 24, 1862, Gatlin ordered an engineer, Captain Richard K. Meade, to the Roanoke River town of Hamilton to design a fort that would eventually become Fort Branch.[243] Gatlin had no further options with regard to the Roanoke River situation.

Shortly after Leventhorpe's Thirty-fourth North Carolina arrived on the Roanoke, a mild stir arose when the War Department ordered Colonel William J. Clarke, commander of the Twenty-fourth North Carolina, to report to General Huger and to assume command of the forces near Weldon. Clarke, at General Robert E. Lee's suggestion, proceeded to order Leventhorpe's newly arrived Thirty-fourth North Carolina Regiment away from the lower Roanoke River to Weldon. None of this activity was reported beforehand to Gatlin, who decried the resulting confusion in his department and resented this intrusion on his authority, even on Lee's orders, without having been conferred with first. Anxious for the safety of the townspeople along the Roanoke, Gatlin countermanded Clarke's order, and Leventhorpe remained on the Roanoke River at Hamilton. Leventhorpe was Burnside's only impediment between the Albemarle Sound and Weldon.[244] The War Department responded by transferring the counties along the Roanoke River—Martin, Halifax, Bertie and Northampton—from Gatlin's command to the Department of Norfolk and transferring Major General William W. Loring from Virginia to command the troops in General Huger's department. Weldon and the Roanoke River thus became General Huger's responsibility.[245]

In Wilmington, General Anderson grew more anxious with anticipation that his Cape Fear District troop numbers were too small to prevent Burnside from swooping down and capturing the port and railhead under his command. Gatlin endorsed Anderson's February 13, 1862 request to the War Department for the return of Clingman's and Radcliffe's regiments that Anderson had loaned to South Carolina in response to the attack on Port Royal.[246] Wilmington would have to wait, however, because Richmond felt that Port Royal still needed Anderson's regiments more. Despite protestations from Jefferson Davis that "the defense of North Carolina occupies my anxious attention"[247] and Secretary Benjamin's assurances that "we are hard at work for you,"[248] the people of North Carolina had reason to believe that the Confederacy intended to sacrifice eastern North Carolina to the Yankees.

With the seeming exception of the Confederate War Department, everybody knew Burnside had a direct bead on New Bern. On March 1, 1862, Gatlin advised the War Department in Richmond of his preparations for defending New Bern and Washington. He ended his report with this plea for reinforcements: "You will perceive that the force under my command is very inadequate to the defense of so extensive a coast against an enemy who has possession of our sounds and can direct his large columns against any point he may elect."[249] Incredibly, on March 2, 1862, the War Department ordered Gatlin's 1,000 troops at Washington, North Carolina, to report to General Randolph in Suffolk, Virginia.[250] In his time of most critical need, Gatlin was stripped of nearly 20 percent of the force within marching distance of New Bern, leaving only about 4,500 men to defend that key port city. Although he complied with the order, Gatlin expressed his displeasure by failing to acknowledge it. Strangely, on March 7, 1862, Governor Clark ordered Gatlin to send Lieutenant Colonel Robert F. Hoke and three of his companies of the Thirty-third North Carolina Regiment to Raleigh. Gatlin at first complied but then abruptly changed his mind and ordered Hoke to remain at New Bern.[251]

On March 8, 1862, Gatlin, his aide and two engineers took the train to New Bern to inspect its defenses and to confer with General Branch. Most communication between Gatlin and Branch was by letter, delivered via the train, because the usual shortages of material and labor had caused long delays in the completion of the telegraph between Goldsboro and New Bern. Ironically, the telegraph line began operation on March 10, 1862, while Gatlin was in New Bern, and buzzed messages for just three days before the Yankees cut it. While Gatlin was consulting with Branch, a recurrence of the malarial-like fever that had plagued him off and on since his days in Indian Territory struck him severely. Compelled to return to Goldsboro and confined to bed by physician Dr. Wyatt Brown, Gatlin was precluded from personally commanding the defense of New Bern.[252] He had no choice but to depend on the relatively inexperienced General Branch, one of Jefferson Davis's civilian appointees.

The very day that Gatlin returned to Goldsboro, March 11, 1862, Burnside departed Roanoke Island with an estimated twelve thousand battle-hardened troops and rendezvoused at Hatteras with thirteen heavily armed gunboats commanded by Commodore Rowan. On March 12, the Union fleet laid anchor in the Neuse River near the mouth of Slocum's Creek, only about twelve miles south of New Bern, and opened the morning of March 13 by bombarding the shores of North Carolina with heavy cannon.[253]

In a fog and drizzle, the three full brigades of Union infantry, commanded by Generals Foster, Reno and Parke, cautiously deployed to shore with their artillery and began the march toward New Bern. Awaiting that Union force just south of New Bern was General Branch with an estimated four thousand untrained and ill-equipped Confederate troops. Most of the Confederate fighters were still awaiting issuance of their military uniforms, and most made do with recently received second-class muskets and antiquated flintlocks or their own assorted sporting rifles and shotguns. On the other hand, most of the Union troops carried modern Springfield and Enfield rifles, both of which fired the deadly minié ball.[254]

In Goldsboro, Gatlin received word of the invasion on March 13, 1862, and immediately wired the War Department of the emergency. Secretary Benjamin ordered the two North Carolina regiments from South Carolina to proceed to New Bern, and Gatlin called for General Anderson to hasten to Goldsboro from Wilmington. He sent Anderson on to Richmond with a written report and a request for large reinforcements and called for another regiment from Wilmington.

On March 14, 1862, although under-equipped and outmanned by a force nearly three times their number, the Confederate soldiers in New Bern

Federal troops occupying captured Confederate fortifications near New Bern in March 1862. *North Carolina Archives.*

fought for four hours before a break in Branch's defensive line precipitated their retreat from the field. Branch had perhaps inadvertently deviated from Gatlin's defensive plan by leaving a 150-yard gap in his line along the railroad at a brick kiln with only a militia unit to cover it. The Yankees quickly probed the weakness, routed the militia unit, penetrated the gap and then simply flanked the Confederates, surrounding and capturing the left wing of the New Bern defenders.[255]

The remaining Confederate army, now overwhelmed, began a hasty and disorganized retreat to the nearest point of refuge, the town of Kinston, some thirty-five miles west. According to D.H. Hill Jr.'s account, Gatlin had issued an order from Goldsboro that secondary lines of defense be constructed so that the inexperienced troops, should they have to retreat, would have defensible positions awaiting them. Hill says that Gatlin's order was not obeyed, perhaps due to the scarcity of available labor, so when the Confederate troops did retreat, it became a "disorderly" rout.[256] Some remnants of Branch's tattered army managed to reach the train depot at Tuscarora and ride, while others scrambled through the Dover Swamp to safety. Colonel Zebulon Vance's Twenty-sixth North Carolina, with Lieutenant Colonel Henry Burgwyn leading the way, escaped across the Trent River to Trenton and worked its way to Kinston. General Branch lost 68 men killed, 116 wounded and 400 captured or missing compared to Burnside's 90 killed, 385 wounded and just 1 man captured. Branch also lost scores of irreplaceable cannon and virtually all of the camp equipment and ammunition stores at New Bern.[257]

That day, March 14, 1862, sixty-five miles to the west, at Goldsboro, General Gatlin shook off the fever that had gripped him for days. He arose hoping to augment Branch's meager force at New Bern and to rally his tiny army. He received word later that day, by train, that New Bern had fallen and that General Branch and the army were in retreat toward Kinston. Gatlin ordered Colonel James H. Lane of the Twenty-eighth North Carolina to assume command of all the troops in the Goldsboro area and to proceed with them to Kinston.[258] In a letter to Adjutant General Cooper, Gatlin advised that he would hold the line near Kinston and consult with General Lee regarding the best positioning of troops for that defense. He also told Cooper, "My health for some time past has not been such as to warrant my taking the field, and for a few days past have been confined to my room; otherwise I should have been present to have conducted the operations in person."[259]

Now, four thousand brave but beaten men rendezvoused by degrees at the town of Kinston, the nearest place of refuge inland from New Bern. The Confederates needed to regroup speedily in order to ward off the Federal advance that surely was on its way. Like virtually all North Carolinians, Gatlin was stunned and angered at the now very real nightmare of Yankees occupying his state. Yet unlike so many who were less pragmatic and more cavalier, he had not discounted that probability. For seven long months, to no avail, he had doggedly warned the Confederate War Department and Governor Henry Clark of the imminent danger and had repeatedly implored them to supply him the means to fight off a coming invasion. The following day, March 15, Gatlin received a telegram from Adjutant General Samuel Cooper of the Confederate War Department in Richmond. Still shaky from days of fever, Gatlin read that he had been relieved of command of the Department of North Carolina and that his subordinate, General Joseph Reid Anderson, had replaced him as commander. Just eight days later, on March 23, 1862, Major General T.H. Holmes replaced Anderson as the Department of North Carolina commander.

During the weeks following the Battle of New Bern, the Confederate government, finally awakening to the crisis and fearing that Burnside would press his advantage westward to the Wilmington & Weldon Railroad, or even to Raleigh, sent nearly twenty-five thousand troops and some of its battle-seasoned generals to Kinston. In addition to General Holmes taking command, Brigadier General Samuel French was dispatched to Kinston and then to Wilmington, where he assumed General Anderson's post as commander of the District of Cape Fear. Holmes had the direct attention of General Robert E. Lee, with whom he corresponded almost daily regarding the situation in eastern North Carolina. Four full brigades of Confederate infantry ultimately made up the Confederate force in the Kinston/

Goldsboro area, with Gatlin's former subordinates, Branch and Anderson, commanding two of them. Brigadier General Robert Ransom and Brigadier General John G. Walker commanded the other two.[260] Had the Confederate government unleashed this large force earlier, it is probable that Burnside would not have invaded North Carolina, and the entire outcome of the war might have changed.

The town of Kinston, which, until the fall of New Bern, had been a sleepy little farming village on the rail line between Goldsboro and New Bern, became the focus of Confederate activity in North Carolina. Thousands of butternut and gray-clad soldiers, from generals to privates, jammed the streets and bivouacked in and just outside of town. With the Confederate army in its midst, Kinston became and would remain an armed camp for three long years. The alarmed townspeople were not enthusiastic about hosting the Confederate soldiers but were relieved to have them, for fear of the Yankee army just thirty-five miles away. The broad, flat piney woods and swampy plain between Kinston and New Bern became a no-man's land, one day held by the Union and the next day by the Confederacy.

With its earlier conquests at Hatteras Inlet and Roanoke Island under tight rein, and with New Bern now under control, the Yankee army had effectively severed eastern North Carolina from the rest of the South. Suddenly freed slaves streamed to New Bern seeking Union harbor from erstwhile bondage, while panic-stricken white North Carolinians across the Coastal Plain and Piedmont fled inland toward safety. However, Burnside did not press his advantage westward beyond New Bern. He was not confident of his ability to take and hold Goldsboro without a better supply line, especially in light of the large increase in Confederate strength coming into North Carolina. Instead, he turned his attention to securing eastern North Carolina's key coastal towns of Washington, Morehead City and Beaufort before subduing Fort Macon in a brief siege on April 25, 1862, and then occupying Plymouth in May. With the sounds and northeastern coast of North Carolina tightly controlled by Federal army and navy rendering Norfolk of little further use to it, the Confederacy abandoned it on May 10, 1862.[261]

After March 15, 1862, the defense of Confederate-held eastern North Carolina would fall to someone other than General Richard C. Gatlin. Following the Battle of New Bern, the Confederate Department of North Carolina would undergo several boundary and leadership changes, and a virtual parade of generals—Joseph R. Anderson, T.H. Holmes, D.H. Hill, Gustavus W. Smith, Samuel G. French, James Longstreet, W.H.C. Whiting, George Pickett and P.G.T. Beauregard—would eventually succeed Gatlin as

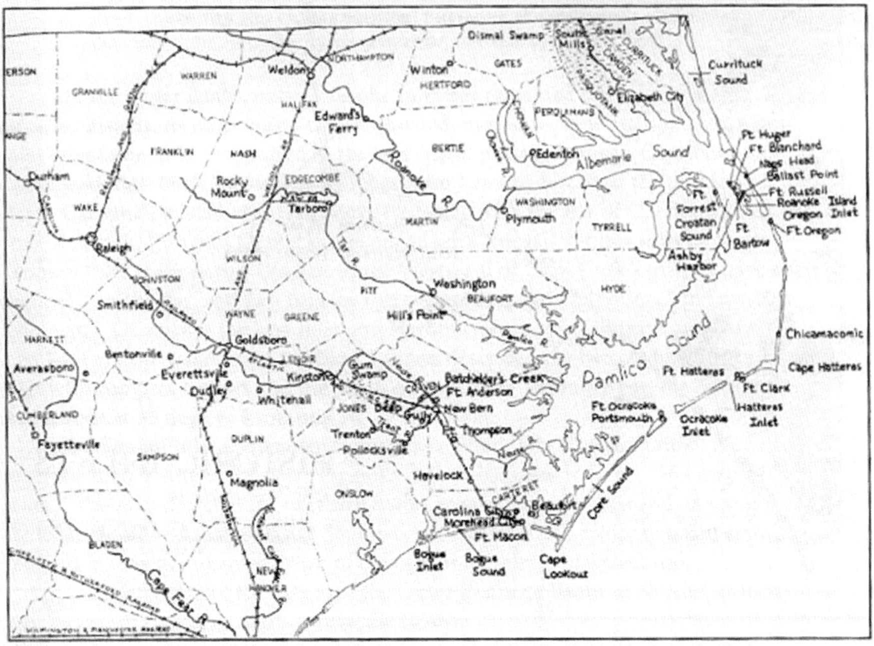

A map of eastern North Carolina taken from John G. Barrett's *North Carolina as a Civil War Battleground*. *North Carolina Archives.*

department commander. Ironically, the Union army, not the Confederacy, found itself defending much of eastern North Carolina after the Battle of New Bern.

The Confederate presence at Kinston prevented Burnside from making a serious move toward inland North Carolina, thus ensuring continued operation of the Wilmington & Weldon Railroad. After securing New Bern, subduing Fort Macon and occupying the town of Washington, Burnside departed North Carolina in July 1862, leaving General John G. Foster in command. During the summer of 1862, most of the Confederate soldiers at Kinston returned to Virginia. Emboldened, Burnside's successor, General Foster, made one foray inland, burning the Wilmington & Weldon Railroad bridge at Goldsboro in December 1862 before retreating to New Bern. Along the way, Foster encountered stiff resistance from General Nathan Evans at the First Battle of Kinston.

During the three years following the Burnside Expedition, the Confederates launched several attempts from Kinston to recapture New Bern, but none was successful. Kinston became headquarters for

Confederate generals Robert Ransom, Samuel French, D.H. Hill, Robert F. Hoke, P.G.T. Beauregard, George Pickett and Braxton Bragg and all of their armies before finally being captured by Union general Schofield in the closing days of the war in March 1865 following the Battle of Wyse Fork.

Engineer Walter Gwynn returned to North Carolina in 1863 as a Confederate colonel and engineered Kinston's batteries on the Neuse River. General Whiting returned to North Carolina as commander of Fort Fisher and died in 1865 of wounds received there. Governor Clark did not run for reelection in 1862, and the people elected the colonel of the Twenty-sixth North Carolina, Zebulon Vance, in his place. General Martin gave up the adjutant general's post for a field command in Virginia and closed out the war as commander of the Western District of North Carolina. General Anderson received a wound in July 1862 at the Battle of Frayser's Farm while commanding his brigade in Virginia. He returned to Richmond as a civilian to resume direction of the Tredegar Iron Works. General D.H. Hill went on to become one of Lee's most distinguished and most temperamental fighters.

General Branch, while commanding a brigade in Virginia, took a fatal sniper's bullet at Antietam on September 17, 1862. General Huger, after abandoning Norfolk to the Federals in 1862, found himself on ordnance duty for the remainder of the war. General Wise took a year to recover his health and then went on to perform superb service as a field commander in Florida and Virginia. General Holmes served only briefly as commander of the North Carolina Department. President Davis soon transferred him to the Trans-Mississippi and promoted him to lieutenant general. He ended the war in state service as head of the North Carolina reserves. General Burnside was responsible for the Union loss and heavy casualties at Fredericksburg in November 1862 and never achieved the success predicted of him.

Chapter 14

"These Failures Do Not by Right Rest with Me": After the Fall

Upon accepting command of the Confederate Department of North Carolina in August 1861, Gatlin's plan for protecting North Carolina from Union invasion was to seal off the coastline with Confederate gunboats; deploy troops at key locations on the Outer Banks, at New Bern, at Fort Macon and below Wilmington; and maintain a sizable reserve of troops at the railroad junction in Goldsboro that could be sent by rail to any point of attack. On paper, this was a sound and workable plan. Then, for six months, he demanded, cajoled, begged and pleaded with both the North Carolina governor and the Confederate War Department to furnish the soldiers, weapons and gunboats necessary to protect the very locations that Burnside had just conquered. Instead of strengthening North Carolina, the Confederacy chose to siphon off the bulk of North Carolina's troops to Virginia. President Jefferson Davis and his War Department seemed determined to employ nearly all the South's resources in preventing a Federal romp through the Old Dominion. Gatlin had at his disposal far too few soldiers, and virtually no navy, to guard the entire North Carolina coastline with its vast sounds and myriad rivers and bays against a far superior Yankee army and a dominant fleet of Union warships.

The Confederate War Department might have been anxious to divert attention from its foot-dragging ineffectiveness in North Carolina by replacing Gatlin as commander of the North Carolina Department the day after New Bern fell. Gatlin, however, had inadvertently asked to be relieved by the message he had sent with Anderson to Richmond on March 15, 1862:

> *I dispatched General Anderson to Richmond on the 15th of March, to represent to the President the necessity of sending a force sufficient to cope with that of the enemy, and desired him to say to the President that, not having confidence in my health or ability to command such a force, I hoped a general of superior rank would be sent with the troops.*[262]

Gatlin suffered, first, the disgrace of losing his command and, second, the public scorn all too commonly heaped on a losing commander. In a panic, the North Carolina press howled that Gatlin was to blame for the disastrous defeat—that he was incompetent, had been drunk and was an "incubus" who should be court-martialed and banished from the state.[263] One Northern newspaper went so far as to wrongly report that Gatlin and Branch had been arrested and taken to Richmond for trial.[264]

Gatlin, of course, from March 11, 1862, until the fall of New Bern on March 14, had been bedridden with chills and fever, too incapacitated to lead his troops in battle. Suspecting that his dismissal was due to the local outcry against him rather than because of his illness, he steadfastly refused to allow himself to become a scapegoat for the Confederate War Department. He immediately demanded of the War Department an inquiry into his actions and offered himself for field command elsewhere. Gatlin felt honor-bound to clear the air about his abrupt unseating, especially after Governor Clark sent an accusatory letter on March 15 to Secretary Benjamin impugning Gatlin's sincerity and his practices. In it, Clark said:

> *I hear much complaint and criticism among the people of the absence of General Gatlin from the field of battle and his entire neglect and inattention to the coast defenses of his command for the last five months, and they judge of this neglect and inattention from the alleged fact that he has not during that period visited and examined the fortifications and inspected the troops more than once, if at all, during his command of six months, notwithstanding his headquarters are in easy railroad communication of both Generals Anderson's and Branch's commands.*
>
> *I am only stating what I hear constantly around me. Perhaps his headquarters is the proper place for him, but the people so deeply interested in their own homes and interests expected the benefit of his military knowledge and experience, and* [are] *greatly distressed that they have not had it, and regard with much anxiety his want of attention to their safety and interest and what they believe was his special business.*[265]

Of course, Clark's allegations were without merit because Gatlin had visited and inspected Wilmington, New Bern and Fort Macon on numerous occasions during his command and had negotiated with his superiors in Richmond, past the point of frustration, trying to procure troops and arms with which to safeguard eastern North Carolina. Clark, angry that the Confederacy had failed to provide for North Carolina's defense as promised, might have been chiding the War Department by blaming its appointed general, but he might also have been redirecting attention from himself, for he was not totally blameless for the loss at New Bern. Prior to the battle, Adjutant General Martin had urged the governor to call out ten thousand North Carolina militia troops to help defend New Bern, but Clark refused to do so because he thought the Confederate government should provide that defense.[266] At any rate, Gatlin's anger rose to the point that he demanded a public explanation. Writing to Adjutant General Cooper on March 19, Gatlin complained, "My being relieved at this particular juncture would lead to the belief that it was done in consequence of the fall of New Berne. If such is the case, or if any blame is attached to me for our misfortunes in that quarter, I desire that an investigation be had at the earliest day practicable."[267]

When, by March 28, 1862, Gatlin had heard nothing from the War Department, he again wrote to Cooper:

> *The many false reports and abusive epithets bestowed upon me in the newspapers of this State since the fall of New Berne make me impatient for a reply to my letter of the 19th instant. If I am blamed by the Government for the conduct of affairs in the Department of North Carolina, surely I ought to be heard in my defense. On the contrary, if my conduct is approved common justice demands that I should be told so. I feel that until this is settled I can render no further service in the Army. I must therefore beg that immediate action be had on the letter referred to.*[268]

Finally, on March 31, 1862, sixteen days after his dismissal, Gatlin received a conciliatory reply from the War Department, this time from yet another new Confederate war secretary, George W. Randolph, essentially brushing the matter aside by saying:

> *I have the honor to inform you that you were relieved from duty on your own official representation that the state of your health was such as to prevent your taking the field. This was the reason assigned in the order relieving*

you of your command, and no reflection has been cast upon you in any communication from this Department.[269]

In April 1862, Gatlin was back in good health. He was still a commissioned brigadier general, so he wrote to the secretary of war again soliciting a field command. As month followed month, Gatlin kept well abreast of war developments, but when no assignment came from Richmond, it appeared the War Department had no further plans for him. Except for an extended trip to Sulphur Springs in Catawba County in the fall, he remained at home in Everettsville with his wife, children and sister. On November 7, 1862, Mary Ann Gatlin gave birth to the couple's third child, a daughter, Sallie Price Perkins Gatlin. By January 1863, Gatlin felt ignored long enough, so he went to Richmond to discuss his situation with Confederate secretary of war James A. Seddon. The meeting resulted in Gatlin's officially resigning his Confederate army commission retroactive to September 8, 1862. In his official report, he stated in his own defense that

we failed to make timely efforts to maintain the ascendancy on the Pamlico Sound, and thus admitted Burnside's fleet without a contest; we failed to put a proper force on Roanoke Island, and thus lost the key to our interior coast; and we failed to furnish General Branch with a reasonable force, and thus lost the important town of New Berne. What I claim is that these failures do not by right rest with me.[270]

By the autumn of 1862, most people had absolved Gatlin of blame or at least publicly forgiven him. Once public emotion calmed and the facts became clear, the press recanted and withdrew the outraged but spurious accusations of drunkenness and incompetence levied against Gatlin. While he might have made the most of limited resources, some still thought he relied too heavily on the energy and expertise of his engineers and subordinate commanders, especially on D.H. Hill, to pursue their own tactics without his direct intervention. Accordingly, some of his staunchest supporters characterized him as "a man of very good sense, but slow, and somewhat wanting in energy"[271] and "a man of very good judgment, but too indolent entirely for such times as these."[272] Perhaps so, but Gatlin's strategy for eastern North Carolina, arguably the soundest that could have been devised, was undermined by a Confederate government preoccupied with defending Virginia and too weak to defend all its country's borders. Gatlin did all in his power to prevent the occupation of eastern North Carolina by Union forces, but with a glaring lack of support from the Confederacy, his command was doomed. Historian Richard A. Sauers claimed that Gatlin "could not have done more for the defense of Newbern."[273] William Trotter states, "Gatlin drew up a sound and thoroughly professional strategy for defending the coast."[274] It was inevitable that eastern North Carolina should have fallen to the superior Union military force, and it is doubtful that even General Robert E. Lee, had he been present and in charge, could have prevented the Yankee capture of eastern North Carolina.

Chapter 15

"I Shall Turn Gurilla": North Carolina Adjutant General

During the Civil War, as now, the North Carolina adjutant general was a cabinet-level post appointed by the state governor. The adjutant general was the state's highest-ranking military officer and carried the militia rank of major general. He commanded the state's militia and executed the governor's directives regarding military affairs. The Civil War elevated the post to one of critical importance even though much of the adjutant general's work was administrative in nature and away from the public eye.

In April 1861, well before North Carolina seceded, Governor John Ellis had agreed to send North Carolina regiments to Virginia. Colonel John F. Hoke, the adjutant general in Ellis's administration, oversaw the creation of short-term volunteer regiments, the first six of which hastened to Virginia. In all, Hoke raised fourteen regiments, designated the First through the Fourteenth North Carolina Volunteer Regiments. But to facilitate raising, arming and training ten long-term regiments called for by the Confederate War Department, the legislature created a second adjutant general post, and Ellis named Brigadier General James G. Martin, a native North Carolinian and a Mexican War veteran, to fill it.[275] In the summer of 1861, Martin, who resigned his U.S. Army brevet major commission on June 14, 1861, raised and trained ten new regiments, designated the First through the Tenth North Carolina State Troops. Due to changing conditions, including the death of Governor Ellis and the impending cession of North Carolina's defense to the Confederate government, the state reorganized its military structure during July and August 1861. The First through the Tenth State Troops retained their regimental number designations. Hoke

A photo of North Carolina Civil War governor Zebulon Vance taken between 1870 and 1880. *Library of Congress.*

resigned to command the Thirteenth North Carolina Volunteer Regiment in the field (later designated the Twenty-third North Carolina), Martin assumed Hoke's duties, the state's coastal defense and troops were turned over to the Confederacy and the Military Board was dissolved. Henry T. Clark, Governor Ellis's successor, consolidated the Quartermaster, Paymaster, Commissary and Ordnance Departments into the adjutant general's office. In November 1861, the First through the Fourteenth North Carolina Volunteers were re-designated as the Eleventh through the Twenty-fourth North Carolina Regiments.

Martin continued his role as adjutant general, but in May 1862, he also assumed active command of a Confederate army brigade headquartered in Kinston. When General Robert E. Lee called Martin's brigade to Virginia in the summer of 1862, it seemed that Martin would have to abandon the adjutant general's post. Martin's success in raising and outfitting troops for Confederate service was laudable, and his administrative skills were unquestioned. However, by law, he could not be in both state and Confederate service.[276] When Zebulon Vance was elected governor in August 1862, succeeding Henry Clark, talk began to circulate that Gatlin would be an ideal choice to replace Martin in Vance's cabinet, should Martin resign. Hopeful of returning to state service in some high-ranking capacity, Gatlin wrote to influential friends, including former governors William A. Graham and David L. Swain and Representative John D. Whitford, indicating his wish to seek the adjutant general's post if it became available. On August 17, 1862, from White Sulphur Springs in Catawba County, Gatlin wrote to Whitford:

> *I came to N.C. to tender my services to her, and even my going into the Confederate Services was a consequence of the transfer of our troops, not a matter of choice on my part…I prefer serving the Old State within its limits where I might be of some use to my friends. I know of no position where I might be of more service than in that of Adjt. Genlcy and for that I am willing to resign my Office in the Confederate Army. As Martin still holds on to his brigade, it is likely that he may vacate the Adjt. Genlcy; in which case I should like to have it…I am willing to do my duty anywhere, but my age and former position does not permit me to take a more subordinate official position…If nothing better can be done I shall turn Gurilla* [sic]*…and being a pretty good rifle shot, should bag more than one of the enemy.*[277]

Gatlin's friends warned him, however, that his unpopularity due to the losses of Hatteras, Roanoke Island and New Bern would make it unlikely for him to receive an appointment from the governor.

Martin finally resigned the adjutant general's post in March 1863, and Governor Vance appointed General Daniel G. Fowle to replace him. Fowle, who, as a lieutenant colonel in the Eighth North Carolina, had been captured when Roanoke Island fell but had been paroled two weeks afterward, served in the adjutant general's post for only five months. He abruptly quit on August 26, 1863, angered when Governor Vance overruled his order that all military correspondence must pass through the adjutant general's office. Years later, Fowle would become governor of North Carolina, but in August 1863, Vance needed an adjutant general. At the urging of Gatlin's friends, Vance wired Gatlin with the offer, and Gatlin immediately accepted. Gatlin hurried by train from Goldsboro to Raleigh and assumed his new post on August 28, 1863. He served as adjutant general for the remainder of the war, until April 19, 1865.

The most visible of the adjutant general's duties was his command of the state militia and the Home Guard. All able-bodied white males between the ages of eighteen and forty-five not in Confederate service were liable for militia service. When Gatlin had commanded the Department of North Carolina, calling out the militia was a responsibility jealously guarded by Governor Clark and Adjutant General Martin. Gatlin and his subordinate generals had called out the militia only with permission from the governor's office and only for emergency military service. Following the April 16, 1862 Confederate Conscription Act, which required most white males between the ages of eighteen and thirty-five (later changed to forty-five) to enroll in Confederate service, the militia stayed busy ensuring that conscripts reported for duty and rounding up non-compliers. Enlistments due to the Conscription Act cut deeply into the ranks of militia, leaving only militia officers and anyone exempt from conscription. The Guard for Home Defense, or Home Guard, as it was more commonly known, had been created by the North Carolina legislature on July 7, 1863, to provide for local defense, guard bridges, enforce the conscription act and especially to do something the North Carolina courts had ruled the militia could not do: round up deserters. The Home Guard included all white males aged eighteen to fifty who were exempt from Confederate service. When Gatlin became adjutant general, the Home Guard had existed for only a month, so it developed mostly during Gatlin's command.

The Adjutant General Records in the North Carolina State Archives show that Gatlin began issuing directives and answering inquiries from the various local Home Guard and militia commanders as early as September 2, 1862.[278] Typical inquiries concerned Home Guard organizational rules, the eligibility of certain persons for promotion within the militia and requests for exemption from the Confederacy's conscription act. Although Governor Vance gave Gatlin leeway to interpret, judge and respond to these cases, Vance maintained control over the militia, especially the remaining militia officers, not allowing the Confederacy to conscript them into service. Vance directed the activities of the militia and Home Guard utilizing Gatlin as his enforcer. For example, in November 1864, Gatlin relayed to General Collett Leventhorpe, commander of the Piedmont and Eastern Home Guard brigades, that "the governor wishes you to remain in Kinston."[279] Gatlin answered incoming Home Guard and militia inquiries individually, firmly

The North Carolina State Capitol today; little has changed since 1861. Gatlin served here as adjutant general under Vance in 1863–65. *North Carolina Archives.*

and precisely. For example, in his first correspondence, he advised Home Guard major W.A. Smith in Smithfield that Smith should not commandeer provisions for his unit but should instead purchase them and send the bill to Major Hogg in the adjutant general's Commissary Department.[280]

There is no evidence that Gatlin ever took active field command of any militia or Home Guard troops—that was not his command style. Rather, he directed by correspondence, relying on the militia and Home Guard brigade commanders to act on his and Governor Vance's orders. Besides, Gatlin was responsible for administering not only the militia and Home Guard but the Quartermaster, Ordnance, Commissary and Paymaster Departments as well. Those duties dictated that he remain in Raleigh most of the time.

Increasing or even maintaining troop strength became alarmingly more difficult for the Confederacy after 1863. Catching and returning deserters to the ranks, a primary role of the Home Guard, became a paramount priority for Governor Vance and, consequently, for General Gatlin. Confident that former Confederate colonel Collett Leventhorpe could effectively lead the Home Guard in that effort, Gatlin recommended to Vance that he appoint Leventhorpe to brigadier general in command of the Piedmont and Eastern North Carolina Home Guard. Leventhorpe had been wounded at

Gettysburg; captured on July 5, 1863; and exchanged and paroled on March 9, 1864.[281] Still in recovery, he had resigned his Confederate commission on April 27, 1864, and had returned to his home in Rutherfordton, North Carolina.[282] Leventhorpe accepted Vance's appointment in September 1864 and, beginning in the troublesome Uwharrie Mountain region of Randolph and Moore Counties, aggressively carried out Gatlin's order to "arrest all who aid & abet deserters."[283] Vance desired that Randolph and surrounding counties be cleared of deserters by the end of September, so Leventhorpe, with no time to waste, incarcerated family members who refused to turn in their deserter kinfolk, apparently with Gatlin's approval. In November 1864, Leventhorpe transferred his headquarters to Kinston, where he continued his aggressive duty by executing at least two of the captured deserters.[284] His extreme tactics, although effective, gained widespread notoriety for both himself and Gatlin.

On February 17, 1864, the Confederacy, desperate to fill the declining ranks of its armies by bringing older and younger men into the war, created a new class of conscript—the Reserves. Able-bodied men aged forty-five to fifty formed the Senior Reserves, and boys aged seventeen formed the Junior Reserves. The Reserves were obligated to serve only within their states of residence, ostensibly to free regular soldiers in their states for service elsewhere if needed. It took a couple months to put the Reserves in motion in North Carolina, and it was not until April 18, 1864, that Governor Vance assigned a general to lead them. That general was none other than Gatlin's old friend T.H. Holmes. Holmes had served with varying degrees of success and failure as commander of the Aquia District in Virginia, the North Carolina Department after Gatlin, the Trans-Mississippi Department and the Arkansas District. Returning to North Carolina in early spring 1864, he was, like Gatlin, more eager by this time to serve his home state directly than to serve elsewhere in the Confederacy. In North Carolina, the Confederate conscription officer, Major Peter Mallett, enrolled the Reserves and then turned them over to General Holmes for training and deployment.[285] Gatlin, Holmes and Mallett coordinated their efforts in raising and retaining troops for both North Carolina and Confederate service for the remainder of the war, but control of the Reserves remained clearly with Holmes and Mallett, while control of the militia and Home Guard remained clearly with Governor Vance and Gatlin.

Another burning issue facing Gatlin was the impressment of slaves and free blacks. One of the first things Gatlin did as adjutant general was to issue statewide orders impressing two thousand male slaves and free blacks aged fifteen to fifty to build fortifications at Wilmington and Fayetteville. His instructions were for the militia to choose the workers by equitable assessment from among slave owners, collect the workers and deliver them to the work sites for terms not to exceed two months.[286] Many militia officers wrote to the governor with reports of balky owners and with questions about assessments. Gatlin enforced the orders firmly with directives to use military force where necessary but gave strict orders not to abuse the citizens. Typical of his directives was this on November 25, 1864, to Colonel W.J. McLain of the Eighty-second North Carolina Militia in Walkersville, North Carolina:

> *Where the overseers refuse to let their slaves come you must use force and take them. Those free negroes who are mechanics working at their trade for the good of the community may be exempted. No money can be paid in lieu of labor, it is the labor & not the money that we want. You were to have had the negroes in Salisbury on the 25th Oct. Why have you delayed so long in attending to it? It is expected when orders are issued from this office that they be immediately and faithfully executed.*[287]

Also, this to Colonel Edward Dolby of the Forty-third North Carolina Militia in Tranquility, North Carolina, a few days later:

> *Messrs James A. Crews, Wm M. Lyon, John W. Lyon and Thos B Lyon complain that you have impressed their slaves not in accordance with Special Order No. 102…You will inquire into this matter and if you find that injustice has been done, you will correct it by having the slaves or slave replaced at Wilmington by assessment on those who should have furnished, and returned the replaced slaves to their owners…Mr. Crews also states that the Militia Officers who impressed his slaves told him that if they had your orders to cut his throat, they would do so. Please admonish your officers against using threats of any sort against peaceable citizens, more particularly, such of so inviting a character.*[288]

Some of Gatlin's work as adjutant general included compiling and presenting periodic accounts to Governor Vance. His semiannual report of May 16, 1864, for the fiscal six months of October 1, 1863, through March 31, 1864, thoroughly details expenditures and personnel for the Home Guard, the North Carolina State Troops, the Adjutant's Roll of Honor, the Quartermaster Department, the Subsistence Department and the Ordnance Department.

The Home Guards were primarily involved in capturing deserters and recusant conscripts, as well as providing local defense in the absence of state militia and Confederate troops. The North Carolina State Troops were under direct command of the Confederate field generals but were raised and clothed by the state. The Quartermaster Department furnished clothing, camp and garrison equipage, pay, bounty and transportation for state troops and also supplied clothing to the Confederacy. The Subsistence Department furnished provisions to the troops in state service. The Ordnance Department furnished arms, ammunition and accoutrements to the troops, Home Guard and militia; sold niter and sulfur to Raleigh powder mills; and sold powder to the Confederacy.

It was significant that North Carolina was the only Confederate state to clothe its own troops for the entire war. It was even more significant that North Carolina, under Vance's direction and Gatlin's management, provided over half the Confederacy's food and clothing during the final two years of the war. State-sponsored blockade running, especially by the blockade runner *Ad-Vance*, which began its stealthy voyages to and from Wilmington just prior to Gatlin's tenure and continued under his management until it was captured in the summer of 1864, accounted for much of North Carolina's surplus of clothing and supplies. As blockade running became less dependable, Gatlin had to manage the state's manufacturing outputs more closely. For example, when Confederate quartermaster general Alexander Lawton requisitioned Gatlin for North Carolina's woolen goods, Gatlin refused, citing the probable unreliability of future imports as his reason.[289] To help manage the huge supply-and-demand management of North Carolina's wartime goods and services, Gatlin was fortunate to have inherited for his staff the services of Major John Devereux as quartermaster and Major Thomas D. Hogg as commissary and ordnance officer. Gatlin entrusted the operation of the quartermaster, commissary and ordnance functions to these two, running interference for them and making Vance's directives known to them.[290]

In addition to overseeing the operations of these departments, Gatlin was responsible for reporting balance sheets and preparing budgets. This he attended to very well, as the Adjutant General Records show. For the six-month period of October 1, 1863, through March 31, 1864, Gatlin and Major Hogg actually turned a profit in the Ordnance Department by buying powder from Raleigh mills and reselling it to the Confederacy, while simultaneously providing adequate powder and arms to the troops still on duty in the state.[291]

One of the most important tasks Gatlin accomplished was compiling the numbers of troops supplied by North Carolina during the war. His very detailed and meticulous accounts showed that as of September 30, 1864, North Carolina had transferred 64,636 state troops to Confederate service. It had also provided 18,585 conscripts aged eighteen to forty-five; had sent 21,608 volunteers since the original transfer; and had 3,203 troops in state service, 4,217 Junior Reserves and 5,686 Senior Reserves for a total of 117,935 men, approximately one-seventh of the total Southern force. His later count toward the end of the war shows over 125,000 North Carolinians in service. Historians are much in his debt for his having provided these numbers. The Adjutant General Letter Books, Militia Letter Books, Quartermaster's Records and State Troops Records of 1863 through 1865 at the North Carolina Office of Archives and History were compiled principally by Gatlin and his staff and reflect the breadth and scope of his efforts.

When Gatlin accepted the adjutant general's post in 1863, he relocated his family to Raleigh. Susie was then almost six years old, Richard was three and little Sallie was not yet a year old. Less than a year later, on June 23, 1864, Sallie, not yet two years of age, died of unspecified cause. Gatlin and Mary Ann took Sallie's little body to the Red House Plantation graveyard near Kinston and buried her next to Gatlin's sister Catherine Reavis, close to Gatlin's parents.[292]

During the final six months of the war, General Lee's army faced General Ulysses S. Grant's siege in Petersburg, Virginia, and General Joseph E. Johnston's army tried to hold back General William T. Sherman's northward push out of Georgia. In North Carolina, the Federals targeted Wilmington, attacking Fort Fisher in December 1864 and again in January 1865. The Home Guard and Reserves were essentially North Carolina's last line of defense. Vance made Leventhorpe's Home Guards available to General Braxton Bragg in Wilmington to assist in its defense while Holmes split his Reserves, with some in Wilmington and others struggling to keep the Wilmington & Weldon Railroad in operation near Weldon. General James G. Martin had also returned to North Carolina and commanded, under General Holmes, Reserves in the western part of the state. Fort Fisher fell in February 1865, Sherman swept across South Carolina and into North Carolina in March and the Union armies moved inland from New Bern and Wilmington. Vance managed to keep the state's government intact and operating as normally as possible, while Gatlin and Holmes pressed the Home Guard and Reserves into Confederate service as a last resort. Sherman captured Fayetteville on March 11, 1865, and continued northward toward the railroad juncture at Goldsboro. General Bragg and his declining Confederate brigades intercepted the Union armies from Wilmington and New Bern near Kinston on March 7, 1865, and delayed them in a three-day battle at Wyse Fork before retreating toward Raleigh. General Johnston clashed with Sherman south of Raleigh at Averasboro on March 16 and then retreated and faced Sherman again at the climactic Battle of Bentonville from March 19 through March 21. Following the Battle of Bentonville, Sherman marched part of his army into Goldsboro, while Johnston retreated toward Raleigh, hoping to join with Lee's southbound army and face Sherman with a united Confederate army.

With Sherman's approach, Governor Vance and the other members of North Carolina's state government began preparing for the eventuality of

Richard C. Gatlin, circa 1880. *U.S. Army Heritage and Education Center.*

surrender and loss of the war. In late March and early April, Vance sent many of the state's records to Statesville for safekeeping.[293] On April 11, 1865, even as the Union army neared Raleigh, Gatlin continued the mundane business of the adjutant general by issuing Special Order Number 74, extending by thirty days the leave of W.H.H. Tucker of the Wake County Home Guard.[294] It was his final order. That same day, on Vance's orders, he and State Treasurer Jonathan Worth loaded the state's remaining official records and documents aboard a Greensboro-bound train for safekeeping. Then, around midnight, they left on that train for Greensboro. Governor Vance remained in his office as long as he dared and then also vacated Raleigh at midnight on April 12 for General Hoke's camp a few miles west of Raleigh. The next day, Sherman's Union army moved in to occupy the state capital peacefully.[295]

West of Raleigh, things did not go well. Lee had surrendered to Grant on April 9, 1865, and remnants of Lee's defeated army streamed southward into North Carolina. Looters stole cloth and clothing from the state's supply in the town of Graham, so on April 13, Gatlin hastened to Graham to investigate. He transferred much of the remaining clothing to Greensboro, but upon arriving back in Greensboro on April 15, he found marauding remnants of Lee's defeated army breaking into the warehouses there as well.[296] The state's supply warehouses seemed like fair game to the former Confederate soldiers and to the destitute and hungry civilians who had poured in from the countryside. Gatlin briefly tried to protect the cache of state goods in the Greensboro warehouses, but he and others charged with guarding the state's supplies soon gave way to the looting of the riotous mob that broke into the warehouses and took what they wanted, mostly clothing. There was nothing left for Gatlin to do at that point. His role in the war had ended.

Chapter 16

"My Former Military Life Has Not Peculiarly Fitted Me for a New Occupation": Return to Fort Smith

Gatlin returned to his home in Raleigh on April 19, 1865, and awaited whatever fate would befall him and his family. As a highly respected former U.S. Army officer, the occupying army treated him and his family with civility. Johnston surrendered to Sherman at the Bennett House in Durham on April 26, 1865, and the war was over. Gatlin assumed that his transition back to United States citizenship was a mere formality. Having never been a rabid secessionist, he was anxious after the war to receive his pardon and proceed with a new way of life. He submitted an amnesty application on June 8, 1865, explaining that he had reluctantly served the Confederacy, preferring to remain in service to his home state, to which he felt acute loyalty. He explained that the circumstance placing him in Confederate service was tangential to his desire to serve North Carolina and vowed his restored loyalty to the Stars and Stripes.

However, Gatlin learned to his surprise that special provisions prevented him from receiving general amnesty and that he was required to make special application for pardon to President Andrew Johnson. He fell into three of fourteen special categories excepting persons from general amnesty: (1) he was a Confederate officer above the rank of colonel, (2) he was a West Point graduate who sided with the South and (3) he had resigned his Federal army commission to serve the Confederacy. North Carolina's postwar acting governor, W.W. Holden, recommended that President Johnson suspend Gatlin's pardon indefinitely. Like so many other American army officers who had opted to take

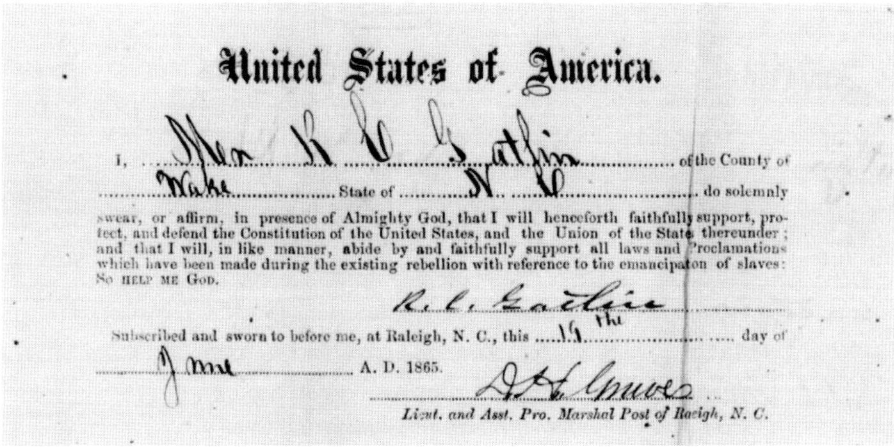

United States of America.

I, Gen R C Gatlin of the County of Wake State of N C do solemnly swear, or affirm, in presence of Almighty God, that I will henceforth faithfully support, protect, and defend the Constitution of the United States, and the Union of the States thereunder; and that I will, in like manner, abide by and faithfully support all laws and Proclamations which have been made during the existing rebellion with reference to the emancipation of slaves: So help me God.

R. C. Gatlin

Subscribed and sworn to before me, at Raleigh, N. C., this 14th day of June A. D. 1865.

D. H. Graves

Lieut. and Asst. Pro. Marshal Post of Raleigh, N. C.

Richard C. Gatlin's amnesty application. *National Archives.*

up the Southern cause, Gatlin found himself unemployed and permanently barred from the only career he had ever known: the military.[297]

With a young wife and family to support, and an unresolved citizenship status, Gatlin had no immediate prospects in North Carolina. He bid farewell forever to his beloved North Carolina and departed Raleigh in October 1865 for the familiar and friendly environs of Fort Smith, Arkansas, where he and Mary Ann had been married less than nine years earlier. While en route on the Ohio River, Gatlin took time to write to Governor Vance:

> *Steamer* Goldena
> *Ohio River*
> *Oct 23, 1865*
>
> *My dear Governor,*
>
> *I wrote your farewell letter before leaving Raleigh, but I perceive it was not mailed. Hence I avail myself of this opportunity to say that I cannot depart for a new home without expressing my thanks for your repeated kindness and to wish you a long life of health, prosperity, and happiness.*
>
> *We left Raleigh on the 10th inst. and arrived at Cincinnati on the 14th. Since then we have been on the steamer moving slowly in the direction of Cairo, where we will be in a few hours. The delay arises from very low water in the River. Should we find the Ark's in the same condition our trip will be tedious indeed.*

My children were much indisposed before leaving Raleigh, but journey has improved them vastly. Perhaps it is the air of the west that has done it.

I design to settle at Ft Smith, Arks, where I trust to make a support for my family, yet I much fear that my former military life has not peculiarly fitted me for a new occupation. I failed to obtain a pardon, but under existing circumstances I do not now think that I shall be interrupted for the want of it. I can form no idea of the public sentiment towards us in the region, not having heard the subject discussed. I think all are disposed to keep their opinions to themselves.

I would be much pleased to receive an occasional letter from you, and if you ever visit Arkansas, trust that you will not fail to visit me.

My wife joins me in kindest regards to Mrs. Vance & yourself.

Your friend
R.C. Gatlin[298]

In their married lives "the General," as Gatlin was called, and Mary Ann had not remained in one place for longer than two years, but Mary Ann had family in Fort Smith, and Fort Smith had been Gatlin's duty post several times from 1851 to 1857, so it was the nearest thing they had to home now. Traveling by rail and by steamboat, they arrived in November 1865 and boarded temporarily with Mary Ann's half sister and her husband, Elizabeth and Samuel L. Griffith. Mary Ann and Elizabeth's mother, Sallie Nicks Gibson, had died in 1863, leaving a fairly sizeable estate, part of which included a small plantation named Oakland Farm about three miles north of Fort Smith on the Sebastian County side of the Arkansas River across from the town of Van Buren. Sam and Elizabeth Griffith sold their share of Oakland Farm to Gatlin in January 1866. With no other apparent options, at age fifty-seven, Gatlin began his new life farming small grains and raising chickens at Oakland Farm. He and his brother-in-law, Robert Gibson, also opened a ferry service across the Arkansas River to Van Buren.

Gatlin continuously and vigorously pursued his pardon from President Johnson after moving to Arkansas. Finally, perhaps acquiescing to an intensive letter-writing campaign and recommendations from several prominent Arkansans and Surgeon General Joseph K. Barnes, the president's Pardons Department granted Gatlin his full pardon on June 25, 1867.[299]

In 1881, seventy-two-year-old Richard Caswell Gatlin retired from farming and moved his remaining family to a house at 923 North Sixth Street in Fort Smith. In Fort Smith, they attended Saint John's Episcopal Church and

R.C. Gatlin Monument, Fort Smith National Cemetery, Fort Smith, Arkansas. *Photo by Eric Leonard. Author's collection.*

visited with old friends from the prewar days. In retirement, Gatlin actively served in local affairs as a member of the local immigration board and as a judge for local talent contests. He undoubtedly was acquainted with another Fort Smith resident, famous "Hanging Judge" Isaac Parker. Parker ruled Fort Smith's court with a stern hand from 1871 until 1896.

Gatlin's old friend from the Seventh Infantry, Benjamin L.E. Bonneville, lived in Fort Smith after the Civil War also. From 1877 until 1884, D.H. Hill served as president of the University of Arkansas–Fayetteville, a short ride north of Fort Smith. It is likely that Gatlin and Hill met on occasion to discuss old times.

Gatlin and Mary Ann had seven children. Only the eldest, Susie, who died in 1904, and the youngest, a daughter named Mary Knox Gatlin, born on May 23, 1875, when Gatlin was sixty-seven years old, lived past childhood.[300]

When Gatlin's sister Mary Gatlin Knox died in Del Norte County, California, in 1890, Gatlin was eighty-one years old. He could look back on simpler days of nearly a century before, when he and others mingled on the banks of the lazy and muddy Neuse River in eastern North Carolina. He could recall the days of horses and steamboats, before railroads and telegraphs and long before the new-fangled telephone and electric lights came along—days when people still spoke the names of Jefferson and Madison and when society seemed somehow more genteel.

Gatlin died on September 8, 1896, at age eighty-seven while visiting Mount Nebo in Yell County, Arkansas. Mount Nebo, situated on a bluff 1,470 feet above the Arkansas River and less than one hundred miles east of Fort Smith, was then the site of a resort spa, a retreat for the politically connected, the well-to-do and the weary steamboat traveler. Gatlin might have gone to Mount Nebo in hopes of recovering from some ailment, he might have been visiting some distant Gatlin relatives or he might have gone simply for a vacation. Whatever the case, he was sick for six days before finally succumbing to colitis. Mary Ann, Susie and Susie's husband, John Corley, were with Gatlin when he died. After interring him at the Fort Smith National Cemetery beside his first wife, Scioto, and his infant son, Alfred Sandford Gatlin, his family marked his grave site with a tall granite obelisk carved with crossed sabers to symbolize his long and outstanding army service.

Richard C. Gatlin, circa 1890. *Courtesy of Caswell Cooke.*

Mary Ann Gibson Gatlin, date unknown. *Courtesy of Caswell Cooke.*

The only known public memorial to Richard Caswell Gatlin, a highway marker erected privately in Kinston, North Carolina, in 2013. *Author's collection.*

Epilogue

Gatlin's youngest daughter, Mary Knox Gatlin, who was born at Fort Smith in 1875, married her distant cousin Collier Cobb, a noted University of North Carolina geology professor, on October 27, 1910, in Chapel Hill, North Carolina. She and her mother moved into the Pigeon Roost, Cobb's home on Franklin Street in Chapel Hill, where Mary raised Cobb's three children from his previous marriage.

Mary Ann Gatlin died at her daughter's home in Chapel Hill on December 18, 1916, at age seventy-nine. She was buried beside Gatlin at the Fort Smith National Cemetery. Mary Knox Gatlin Cobb, Gatlin's youngest child, lived to age ninety-seven, dying on March 18, 1973, in Chapel Hill. She was buried at the Old Chapel Hill Cemetery in Orange County, North Carolina, beside Collier Cobb, who had died on November 28, 1934. Neither of Gatlin's surviving daughters had children, so Gatlin has no living descendants.

In a long-overdue tribute to Richard Caswell Gatlin, a group of Kinston and Lenoir County citizens erected a privately funded historical highway marker at the Kinston/Lenoir County Visitors' Center in Kinston, North Carolina, in 2013. The marker recalls Gatlin as Lenoir County's first West Point graduate; a veteran of the Black Hawk, Seminole and Mexican Wars; and Kinston/Lenoir County's only Civil War general.

Notes

Preface

1. Johnson and Holloman, *Story of Kinston*, 118–19, 139.

Prologue

2. Sauers, *Burnside Expedition*, 261–308.
3. Ibid., 116.

Chapter 1

4. Lefler and Newsome, *North Carolina*, 7.
5. Ibid., 49.
6. Johnson and Holloman, *Story of Kinston*.
7. Ibid., Chapter 5.
8. R.C. Gatlin Papers.
9. Fourth Census of U.S. Population, Lenoir County, NC, 1820.
10. King, "Lenoir County, NC—Lenoir County Settlements with the State."

Chapter 2

11. Gatlin, "Letter to John Branch."
12. Blackledge, "Letter to John Branch."
13. WP Papers.
14. Gatlin, "Letter to James W. Barbour."
15. U.S. Military Academy, "Edgar Allan Poe."
16. Barone, "Evolution of the Cadet Disciplinary System."
17. R.C. Gatlin Papers.

Chapter 3

18. Marks, *In a Barren Land*.
19. Eckert, *Twilight of Empire*, 268.
20. Trask, *Black Hawk*.
21. R.C. Gatlin Papers.
22. Ibid.
23. Ibid.
24. Ibid.

Chapter 4

25. Agnew, Fort Gibson, Chapters 2 and 3.
26. Ibid., 89–113.
27. Foreman, *Advancing the Frontier*.
28. Winders, *Mr. Polk's Army*.
29. R.C. Gatlin Papers.
30. National Archives Returns from the Seventh Regiment of Infantry.
31. Gatlin, "Letter to Adjutant General Roger Jones."
32. R.C. Gatlin Papers.
33. Ibid.
34. Ibid.
35. Foreman, *Advancing the Frontier*.
36. R.C. Gatlin Papers.
37. Ibid.
38. Ibid.
39. Foreman, *Advancing the Frontier*.
40. Catlin, *Letters and Notes*.

41. Davis, *Papers of Jefferson Davis*, 381–83.
42. Foreman, *Advancing the Frontier*, 46–47.
43. Foreman, *Pioneer Days*, 169.
44. Agnew, *Fort Gibson*, 144–45; Foreman, *Pioneer Days*, 161.
45. Laumer, *Massacre*.
46. National Archives Returns from the Seventh Regiment of Infantry.
47. Mahon, *History of the Second Seminole War*.
48. Peters, *Florida Wars*, 108.
49. Laumer, *Dade's Last Command*.
50. Peters, *Florida Wars*, 108.
51. Nester, *Age of Jackson*, 186.
52. National Archives Returns from the Seventh Regiment of Infantry.
53. R.C. Gatlin Papers.
54. Ibid.

CHAPTER 5

55. Lefler and Newsome, *North Carolina*.
56. R.C. Gatlin Papers.
57. Ibid.
58. Ibid.
59. Ibid.
60. Ibid.
61. Ibid.

CHAPTER 6

62. Mahon, *History of the Second Seminole War*.
63. National Archives Returns from the Seventh Regiment of Infantry.
64. Lovell, *Benjamin Bonneville*.
65. R.C. Gatlin Papers.
66. National Archives Returns from the Seventh Regiment of Infantry.
67. Mahon, *History of the Second Seminole War*.
68. Foreman, "Colonel William Whistler."
69. Sprague, *Florida War*.
70. Ibid.
71. Ibid.

72. R.C. Gatlin Papers.
73. Sprague, *Florida War*.
74. R.C. Gatlin Papers.
75. Ibid.
76. National Archives Returns from the Seventh Regiment of Infantry.

CHAPTER 7

77. Nevin, *Mexican War*.
78. *(New Orleans) Picayune*, August 22, 1845.
79. National Archives Returns from the Seventh Regiment of Infantry.
80. Ibid.
81. Ibid.
82. Ibid.
83. Nevin, *Mexican War*.
84. Eisenhower, *So Far from God*.
85. Ferrell, *Monterrey Is Ours!*, 42.
86. Tyndall, *America*.
87. Ibid.
88. Grant, *Personal Memoirs*, 31.
89. Hawkins, "Official Report of Siege of Fort Texas."
90. Nevin, *Mexican War*.
91. Company A, 7th Regiment, United States Infantry, Living History Association.
92. Ferrell, *Monterrey Is Ours!*, 87.
93. Ibid., 127.
94. Ibid., 137.
95. Ibid.
96. Cullum, *Biographical Register*.
97. R.C. Gatlin Papers.
98. Ibid.
99. Ibid.
100. Ibid.
101. Ibid.
102. Givens, *Daniel P. Whiting*, 125.
103. Aztec Club, "Aztec Club."

CHAPTER 8

104. R.C. Gatlin Papers.
105. National Archives Returns from the Seventh Regiment of Infantry.
106. Ibid.
107. Ibid.
108. Ibid.
109. RootsWeb, "GATLIN/L Archive."
110. Ibid.
111. Ferrell, *Monterrey Is Ours!*, xi.
112. Givens, *Daniel P. Whiting*, 125.
113. R.C. Gatlin Papers.
114. Givens, *Daniel P. Whiting*, 135.
115. Jennings, "Useppa Island."
116. National Archives Returns from the Seventh Regiment of Infantry.
117. Ibid.
118. R.C. Gatlin Papers.
119. Tyndall, *America*.
120. National Archives Returns from the Seventh Regiment of Infantry.
121. Foreman, *Advancing the Frontier*.
122. National Archives Returns from the Seventh Regiment of Infantry.
123. Ibid.
124. Foreman, *Advancing the Frontier*.
125. Forrest, "National Pike."
126. R.C. Gatlin Papers.
127. Ibid.
128. *St. Louis Daily Democrat*, February 17, 1854.
129. Engle, *Don Carlos Buell*.
130. R.C. Gatlin Papers.
131. Ibid.
132. Foreman, *Advancing the Frontier*.
133. Ibid.
134. R.C. Gatlin Papers.
135. Foreman, *Advancing the Frontier*.
136. Bearss and Gibson, *Fort Smith*.
137. National Archives Returns from the Seventh Regiment of Infantry.
138. Gatlin, "Letter to Mary Gatlin Knox."
139. Foreman, *Pioneer Days*.
140. R.C. Gatlin Papers.

CHAPTER 9

141. Moorman, *Camp Floyd*, 3–9.
142. National Archives Returns from the Seventh Regiment of Infantry.
143. R.C. Gatlin Papers.
144. Gatlin, "Letter to Mary Gatlin Knox."
145. Ibid.
146. R.C. Gatlin Papers.
147. Ibid.
148. Ibid.
149. Gatlin, "Letter to Mary Gatlin Knox," 1860.
150. R.C. Gatlin Papers.
151. Ibid.
152. Ibid.
153. Gatlin, "Application for Presidential Pardon."
154. Wadsworth, *Incident at San Augustine Springs*.
155. R.C. Gatlin, "Memo to Texas Assistant Adjutant General."
156. R.C. Gatlin Papers.
157. Ibid.
158. *War of the Rebellion: A Compilation of the Official Records of the Union and Confederate Armies* (hereafter *Official Records*), Series 1, vol. 1, 70.
159. Ibid., 650.
160. R.C. Gatlin Papers.

CHAPTER 10

161. Iobst, "North Carolina Mobilizes."
162. Ibid.
163. Trotter, *Ironclads and Columbiads*.
164. Iobst, "North Carolina Mobilizes"; Sauers, *Burnside Expedition*, 83.
165. *Official Records*, Series 1, vol. 51, 146.
166. Ibid., 121.
167. Ibid., 194.
168. Oeffinger, *A Soldier's General*, 87.
169. Hill, *Bethel to Sharpsburg*, 157.
170. *Official Records*, Series 1, vol. 51, 192.
171. Ibid., vol. 4, 633.
172. Ibid., vol. 51, 200.
173. R.C. Gatlin Papers.
174. Ibid.

Chapter 11

175. Clark, *Histories*, 5–6.
176. Sauers, *Burnside Expedition*, 83.
177. *Official Records*, Series 1, vol. 51, 255.
178. Ibid., vol. 4, 636.
179. Ibid., 574; Sauers, *Burnside Expedition*, 88.
180. Trotter, *Ironclads and Columbiads*, 33–41.
181. *Official Records*, Series 1, vol. 51, 260.
182. Ibid., vol. 4, 637.
183. Ibid., vol. 51, 259.
184. Ibid., 263.
185. Ibid., vol. 4, 637.
186. Ibid., 638.

Chapter 12

187. Ibid.
188. Ibid.
189. Ibid., vol. 51, 269.
190. Ibid., vol. 4, 639.
191. Ibid., 649.
192. *Charleston Mercury*, September 12, 1861.
193. R.C. Gatlin, "Letter to Mary Ann Gatlin," 1861.
194. *Official Records*, Series 1, vol. 51, 298.
195. Ibid., vol. 4, 641.
196. Ibid., 656.
197. Ibid., 658.
198. Ibid., 660.
199. Ibid., 662.
200. Ibid., 618.
201. Ibid., vol. 51, 326.
202. Ibid., vol. 4, 662.
203. Ibid., vol. 51, 329.
204. Ibid., vol. 4, 663.
205. *Official Records of the Union and Confederate Navies*, 218.
206. *Official Records*, Series 1, vol. 4, 618.
207. Ibid., 684.
208. Ibid., 682.

209. Ibid., vol. 51, 357.
210. Hill, letter in the *North Carolina Standard.*
211. Davis, *Boy Colonel of the Confederacy*, 89.
212. *Official Records*, Series 1, vol. 4, 705.
213. Ibid., vol. 51, 425.
214. Ibid., vol. 4, 715.

CHAPTER 13

215. *Official Records*, Series 1, vol. 51, 432.
216. Ibid.
217. Ibid., 434.
218. Ibid., 438.
219. Ibid., 439.
220. North Carolina Archives, "Reminiscences: Brigadier General Collett Leventhorpe."
221. *Official Records*, Series 1, vol. 51, 442.
222. Ibid.
223. Ibid., 444.
224. Ibid., 445.
225. Ibid.
226. Ibid., 448.
227. Ibid.
228. *Official Records*, Series 1, vol. 9, 420.
229. Ibid., vol. 51, 452.
230. Ibid., 453.
231. Ibid., vol. 9, 421.
232. Sauers, *Burnside Expedition*, 191; *Official Records*, Series 1, vol. 9, 120.
233. *Official Records*, Series 1, vol. 51, 458.
234. Ibid., vol. 9, 424.
235. Ibid., 426.
236. Ibid.
237. Mallison, *Civil War on the Outer Banks*, 70.
238. Ibid., 70–80; Trotter, *Ironclads and Columbiads*, 75–91.
239. Sauers, *Burnside Expedition*, 200.
240. *Official Records*, Series 1, vol. 9, 121.
241. Ibid., 188.

242. Mallison, *Civil War on the Outer Banks*, 70–80; Trotter, *Ironclads and Columbiads*, 75–99.
243. Shiman, *Fort Branch*, 5.
244. Cole and Foley, *Collette Leventhorpe*, 65.
245. *Official Records*, Series 1, vol. 4, 577; Ibid., vol. 51, 479.
246. Ibid., vol. 9, 432.
247. Ibid., 434.
248. Ibid., 433.
249. Ibid., 441.
250. Ibid., 442.
251. Ibid., vol. 51, 492.
252. Ibid., vol. 9, 443.
253. Sauers, *Burnside Expedition*, 261–308.
254. Ibid.
255. Ibid.
256. Hill, *Bethel to Sharpsburg*, 231.
257. *Official Records*, Series 1, vol. 51, 504.
258. Ibid., vol. 9, 444.
259. Ibid., 443.
260. Ibid., 460.
261. Hill, *Bethel to Sharpsburg*, 40.

Chapter 14

262. *Official Records*, Series 1, vol. 4, 578.
263. *Weekly Raleigh Register*, March 26, 1862.
264. *Richmond Daily Dispatch*, 1862.
265. *Official Records*, Series 1, vol. 9, 445.
266. Clark, *Histories*, 8–9.
267. *Official Records*, Series 1, vol. 51, 506.
268. Ibid., 517.
269. Ibid., vol. 9, 525.
270. Ibid., vol. 4, 578.
271. Williams and Hamilton, *Papers of William Alexander Graham.*
272. Ibid.
273. Sauers, *Burnside Expedition*, 455.
274. Trotter, *Ironclads and Columbiads*, 61.

Chapter 15

275. Clark, *Histories*, 3.
276. Ibid., 10.
277. Gatlin, "Letter to John D. Whitford."
278. Bradley, *North Carolina Confederate Militia*, vol. 3, 1, 3.
279. Ibid., 98.
280. Ibid., 1, 3.
281. Cole and Foley, *Collette Leventhorpe*, 126–27.
282. Ibid., 133.
283. Ibid., 139.
284. Ibid., 145.
285. Hilderman, *Theophilus Hunter Holmes*, Chapter 9.
286. Martinez, *Confederate Slave Impressment*.
287. North Carolina Archives, "Adjutant General Records," 526.
288. Ibid., 530.
289. Wilson, *Confederate Industry*, 113.
290. Armistead, "John Devereux Jr."
291. North Carolina Archives, "Adjutant General Records."
292. R.C. Gatlin Papers.
293. Clark, *Histories*, 55.
294. Bradley, *North Carolina Confederate Militia*, vol. 2, 72, 665.
295. Barrett, *Sherman's March*, 216.
296. Angley, Cross and Hill, *Sherman's March*, 81–82.

Chapter 16

297. Civil War Amnesty Papers.
298. Gatlin, "Letter to Zebulon Vance."
299. Civil War Amnesty Papers.
300. R.C. Gatlin Papers.

Bibliography

Agnew, Brad. *Fort Gibson: Terminal on the Trail of Tears*. Norman: University of Oklahoma Press, 1980.

Angley, Wilson, Jerry L. Cross and Michael Hill. *Sherman's March through North Carolina*. Raleigh: North Carolina Division of Archives and History, 1995.

Armistead, Terrell L. "John Devereux Jr." NCpedia.org. http://ncpedia.org/biography/devereux-john-jr (accessed April 16, 2014).

Aztec Club. "Aztec Club." http://www.aztecclub.com (accessed November 25, 2003).

Barone, Laureen M. "Evolution of the Cadet Disciplinary System: From Confusion to Clarity (1802–1833). HI600, LTC(P) J. Johnson and MAJ A. Care, 4 December 1990." http://digital-library.usma.edu/libmedia/archives/toep/cadet_discipline_sys_confusion_clarity_1802_1833.pdf (accessed March 23, 2014).

Barrett, John G. *Sherman's March through the Carolinas*. Chapel Hill: University of North Carolina Press, 1956.

Bearss, Edwin C., and A.M. Gibson. *Fort Smith: Little Gibraltar on the Arkansas*. Norman: University of Oklahoma Press, 1969.

Blackledge, William. "Letter to John Branch." 1828. U.S. Military and Naval Academies, Cadet Records and Applications, 1805–1908, Ancestry.com.

Bradley, Stephen E., Jr. *North Carolina Confederate Militia and Home Guard Records*. Virginia Beach, VA: self-published, 1995.

Catlin, George. *Letters and Notes on the North American Indians*. New York: Gramercy Books, 1975.

Charleston Mercury. September 12, 1861.

Civil War Amnesty Papers, 1865–1867. August 14, 1867. Fold3. http://www.fold3.com/image/22613572/ (accessed June 07, 2014).

Clark, Walter, ed. *Histories of the Several Regiments and Battalions from North Carolina in the Great War 1861–65*. Vol. 1. Raleigh: State of North Carolina, 1901.

Cole, J. Timothy, and Bradley R. Foley. *Collette Leventhorpe: The English Confederate*. Jefferson, NC: McFarland & Company, 2007.

Company A, 7th Regiment, United States Infantry, Living History Association. http://www.cottonbaler.com (accessed September 15, 2003).

Cullum, Brevet Major General George W. *Biographical Register of the Officers and Graduates of the U.S. Military Academy*. Vol. 1. Boston and New York: Houghton, Mifflin and Co., 1891.

Davis, Archie K. *Boy Colonel of the Confederacy: The Life and Times of Henry King Burgwyn Jr*. Chapel Hill: University of North Carolina Press, 1985.

Davis, Jefferson. *The Papers of Jefferson Davis: Volume 1, 1808–1840*. Edited by Haskell M. Monroe Jr. and James T. McIntosh. Baton Rouge: Louisiana State University Press, 1971.

Eckert, Allan W. *Twilight of Empire*. New York: Bantam Books, 1988.

Eisenhower, John S.D. *So Far from God: The U.S. War with Mexico, 1846–1848*. New York: Random House, 1989.

Engle, Stephen D. *Don Carlos Buell: Most Promising of All*. Chapel Hill: University of North Carolina Press, 1999.

Faust, Patricia L., ed. *Historical Times Illustrated Encyclopedia of the Civil War*. New York: Harper and Row, 1986.

Ferrell, Robert H., ed. *Monterrey Is Ours! The Mexican War Letters of Lieutenant Dana, 1845–1847*. Lexington: University Press of Kentucky, 1990.

Foreman, Carolyn Thomas. "Colonel William Whistler." *Chronicles of Oklahoma* 18, no. 4 (December 1940). http://digital.library.okstate.edu/Chronicles/v018/v018p313.html.

Foreman, Grant. *Advancing the Frontier, 1830–1860*. Norman: University of Oklahoma Press, 1933.

———. *Pioneer Days in the Early Southwest*. Lincoln: University of Nebraska Press, 1994.

Forrest, Earle R. "National Pike, Road of History, Romance." *Washington (PA) Reporter*, March 30, 1955.

Fourth Census of U.S. Population, 1820, Lenoir County, North Carolina.

Gatlin, John. "Letter to John Branch." 1827.

Gatlin, R.C. "Application for Presidential Pardon." June 21, 1865. North Carolina Department of Archives and History.

———. "Letter to Adjutant General Roger Jones." March 3, 1833. Fold3, Letters Received by the Adjutant General, 1822–1860.

———. "Letter to James W. Barbour." 1828. U.S. Military and Naval Academies, Cadet Records and Applications, 1805–1908, Ancestry.com.

———. "Letter to John D. Whitford." August 17, 1862. North Carolina State Archives.

———. "Letter to Mary Ann Gatlin." September 4, 1861. R.C. Gatlin Papers, Southern Collection, UNC–Chapel Hill.

———. "Letter to Mary Gatlin Knox." July 26, 1856. R.C. Gatlin Papers, Southern Collection, UNC–Chapel Hill.

———. "Letter to Mary Gatlin Knox." October 18, 1857. R.C. Gatlin Papers, Southern Collection, UNC–Chapel Hill.

———. "Letter to Mary Gatlin Knox." January 18, 1858. R.C. Gatlin Papers, Southern Collection, UNC–Chapel Hill.

———. "Letter to Mary Gatlin Knox." February 27, 1860. R.C. Gatlin Papers, Southern Collection, UNC–Chapel Hill.

———. "Letter to Zebulon Vance." October 23, 1865. Zebulon Vance Papers, North Carolina State Archives.

———. "Memo to Texas Assistant Adjutant General." March 18, 1861. Undocumented website.

Givens, Murphy, ed. *Daniel P. Whiting: A Soldier's Life*. Corpus Christi, TX: Nueces Press, 2011.

Grant, Ulysses S. *Personal Memoirs of Ulysses S. Grant*. New York: Charles L. Webster & Company, 1884.

Hawkins, Captain Edgar S. "Official Report of Siege of Fort Texas." http://www.dmwv.org/mexwar/documents/fttexas2.htm (accessed November 24, 2003).

Hilderman, Walter C., III. *Theophilus Hunter Holmes: A North Carolina General in the Civil War*. Jefferson, NC: McFarland & Company, 2014.

Hill, Daniel Harvey, Jr. *Bethel to Sharpsburg: A History of North Carolina in the War Between the States*. Vol. 1. Raleigh, NC: Edwards & Broughton Co., 1926.

Hill, D.H. Letter in the *North Carolina Standard*, November 27, 1861.

Iobst, Richard W. "North Carolina Mobilizes: Nine Crucial Months, December 1860–August, 1861." PhD dissertation, University of North Carolina, 1968.

Jennings, James. "Useppa Island." *South Florida History* (Winter 1998–99).

Johnson, Talmadge C., and Charles R. Holloman. *The Story of Kinston and Lenoir County*. Raleigh, NC: Edwards & Broughton Co., 1954.

King, Russell. "Lenoir County, NC—Lenoir County Settlements with the State." USGenWeb Archives. http://ftp.rootsweb.com/pub/usgenweb/nc/lenoir/court/cset.txt.

Laumer, Frank. *Dade's Last Command*. Gainesville: University of Florida Press, 1995.

———. *Massacre: An Account of the Massacre of Major Francis L. Dade and His Men by the Seminole Indians in Florida, December 28, 1835*. Gainesville: University of Florida Press, 1968.

Lefler, Hugh T., and Albert Newsome. *North Carolina: The History of a Southern State*. Chapel Hill: University of North Carolina Press, 1973.

Lovell, Edith Haroldsen. *Benjamin Bonneville: Soldier of the American Frontier*. Bountiful, UT: Horizon Publishers, 1992.

Mahon, John K. *History of the Second Seminole War, 1835–1842*. Gainesville: University of Florida Press, 1985.

Mallison, Fred M. *The Civil War on the Outer Banks*. Jefferson, NC: McFarland & Company, 1998.

Marks, Paula Mitchell. *In a Barren Land: American Indian Dispossession and Survival*. New York: William Morrow Company, 1998.

Martinez, Jaime Amanda. *Confederate Slave Impressment in the Upper South*. Chapel Hill: University of North Carolina Press, 2013.

Moorman, Donald R. *Camp Floyd and the Mormons: The Utah War*. Salt Lake City: University of Utah Press, 1992.

National Archives Returns from the Seventh Regiment of Infantry, Microfilm Group M665, Rolls 78, 79, 80.

Nester, William. *The Age of Jackson and the Art of American Power, 1815–1848*. Dulles, VA: Potomac Books, 2013.

Nevin, David. *The Mexican War*. New York: Time-Life Books, 1978.

(New Orleans) Picayune. August 22, 1845.

North Carolina Archives. "Adjutant General Records, 1863–1865."

———. "Reminiscences: Brigadier General Collett Leventhorpe." Box 71, Folder 20_0018.

Oeffinger, John C., ed. *A Soldier's General: The Civil War Letters of Major General LaFayette McLaws*. Chapel Hill: University of North Carolina Press, 2002.

Official Records of the Union and Confederate Navies During the War of Rebellion. Washington, D.C.: U.S. Government Printing Office, 1897–1917.

Peters, Virginia. *The Florida Wars*. Hamden, CT: Archon Books, 1979.

Richmond Daily Dispatch. April 21, 1862.

RootsWeb. "GATLIN/L Archive." http://archiver.rootsweb.com/th/read/GATLIN/2001-08/0999014769 (accessed September 15, 2003).

Sauers, Richard. *The Burnside Expedition*. Dayton, OH: Morningside Press, 1996.

Shiman, Phillip. *Fort Branch and the Defense of the Roanoke Valley, 1862–1865*. Hamilton, NC: Fort Branch Battlefield Commission, 1990.

Sprague, John T. *The Florida War*. Reproduction of the 1848 edition. Tampa, FL: University of Tampa Press, 2000.

St. Louis Daily Democrat. February 17, 1854.

Trask, Kerry A. *Black Hawk: The Battle for the Heart of America*. New York: Henry Holt and Company, 2006.

Trotter, William. *Ironclads and Columbiads: The Civil War in North Carolina*. Vol. 3. Greensboro, NC: John F. Blair, 1989.

Tyndall, George Brown. *America: A Narrative History*. Vol. 1. New York: W.W. Norton and Co., 1984.

U.S. Military Academy. "Edgar Allan Poe: The Army Years." USMA Library Bulletin 10. http://digital-library.usma.edu/libmedia/archives/bulletins/b10_edgar_poe.pdf (accessed June 01, 2014).

Wadsworth, Richard. *Incident at San Augustine Springs*. Las Cruces, NM: Yucca Tree Press, 2002.

The War of the Rebellion: A Compilation of the Official Records of the Union and Confederate Armies. 128 vols. Washington, D.C.: U.S Government Printing Office, 1880–1901.

Weekly Raleigh Register. March 26, 1862.

Williams, Max R., and J.G. De Roulhac Hamilton, eds. *The Papers of William Alexander Graham: Volume V, 1857–1863*. Raleigh: North Carolina Department of Archives and History, 1973.

Wilson, Harold S. *Confederate Industry*. Jackson: University of Mississippi Press, 2002.

Winders, Richard Bruce. *Mr. Polk's Army*. College Station: Texas A&M University Press, 1997.

Index

Y

About the Author

James L. Gaddis Jr., a Tampa, Florida native, is a retired computer software designer and database administrator, having spent forty-five years with East Carolina University, Mutual of America Insurance Company, Pratt & Whitney Aircraft, Hampton Industries and the U.S. Air Force. Gaddis is president of the Kinston Civil War Round Table and a longtime member of the CSS Ram Neuse Sons of Confederate Veterans Camp 1427 in Kinston, North Carolina. He has spoken at numerous civic and history group functions around eastern North Carolina, including the Museum of the Albemarle's Burnside Expedition Symposium. He served with the U.S. Air Force in Vietnam, earned a bachelor of arts degree in economics from North Carolina State University and completed several graduate courses in history at East Carolina University. Married with two adult children and five grandchildren, Gaddis makes his home in Lenoir County, North Carolina, where some lines of his family have resided since colonial days.